Devil Bait

High Heels & Spiritual Whorefare

Devil Bait

High Heels & Spiritual Whorefare

Tiffany Buckner

Anointed Fire House Christian Publishing
www.anointedfirehouse.com

Copyright Notice
2016

Devil Bait
High Heels & Spiritual Whorefare

© 2016, Tiffany Buckner
Anointed Fire™ House
(info@anointedfire.com)

Anointed Fire
ISBN-13: 978-0998250700
ISBN-10: 0998250708

Dedication

I dedicate this book to the amazing God who set me free from sexual immorality: YAHWEH.

Note from the Author

Dear Reader,

First and foremost, let me thank you for purchasing *Devil Bait: High Heels and Spiritual Whorefare.* This is book number thirty-three and I'm truly excited about its release.

The purpose of this book is to expose the devils lurking behind sexual immorality. If you are familiar with my ministry, then you already know I address demonic spirits and behaviors in both men and women via my books, audio teachings and articles... though my ministry has mainly been tailored towards women. I decided to write this book over a year ago after speaking with a brother in Christ. Like many men, he'd found himself repeatedly in the snares of immoral women and didn't understand why. Having been an immoral woman (before I got saved), I began to educate him on the heart and mindset of the seductress. He was amazed and told me that a lot of men aren't aware of what I'd shared with him. He encouraged me to write a book about it and I said that I would do it someday. I decided to go ahead and start the book at the Lord's urging because a lot of men are unaware of the schemes of the enemy. Many don't know the purpose of an immoral woman.

Not only will this book help men to understand the mindset, skill-set and goals of an immoral woman, it will help men to find their God-appointed wives. It will also help women to understand how Satan trains them to be sexually immoral. This is especially true for single women who want to get married someday. Satan launches attacks on women that are designed to ensure they will never get married. However, if a woman does get married, Satan wants her to expose her husband to him and then lose him.

When reading this book, I want you to revisit your childhood and find every demon that was lurking there; that way, the adult version of you can kick it out of your life once and for all. This book is informative and you will find parts of my testimony throughout the book.

I pray that this book educates, blesses and encourages you. I guarantee that you will never be the same after reading this book!

Your Sister in Christ,
Tiffany Buckner

Table of Contents

Introduction

You log onto your computer, go to your favorite social media platform and discover that your favorite pastor, gospel singer or evangelist is going through a divorce. How could this be? The man in question is full of wisdom, knowledge and understanding; plus, he's preached some really powerful messages about marriage. You reason within yourself that since the wife is behind the scenes and you don't know her character, she must be the problem. *Truthfully, you may want her to be the problem; after all, we need God-fearing, Holy Spirit-filled leaders who can not only preach a message, but live it.* A few weeks later (or immediately after the divorce has been finalized), your social media page is buzzing yet again. Your favorite leader has a new woman on his arm; a woman that, as it turns out, he'd been seeing while he was married; *but* they were just "friends" back then ... *or so they say.* Their friendship seemed to have "budded" into romance the very minute the judge granted the man's divorce. Even if the new couple hadn't been friends during the man's previous marriage, the fact that the woman is ungodly is enough to make you question your discernment. What's going on with him? Why are so many Christian men (including leaders) leaving the wives of their youth to pursue Delilahs, Jezebels and the like? What's swallowing up our young men before they can even find their way into a church? The answer is simple: the gates of hell have opened and warfare has come out of it wearing high heels.

In *Devil Bait: High Heels & Spiritual Whorefare*, you will understand how the seductress is created, what her assignment is and how she leads so many men astray. Additionally, you will read my firsthand account with seduction and how God set me free from that vicious and filthy spirit.

Before You Start Reading

We must remember that the seductress, temptress, adulteress, enchantress, sorceress, whore, Delilah, Jezebel and whatsoever we may call her is first a creation of God. Underneath all the evil that we see, there lies a wounded soul and a broken spirit, and believe it or not, she has a story. Her story is likely filled with heartbreak, betrayal, abandonment, rejection and the like. If you sit down and listen to her story, you will be able to mentally envision her process to demonic discipleship. I always say that even though I regret hurting God and unleashing so much evil in my youth, I thank God that because of who, what and where I was, I now have a compassionate heart towards all women, including immoral women. This enables me to effectively lead many broken souls back to the God.

Additionally, ever since I started in deliverance ministry, I've gained a new level of compassion for immoral women. I've heard so many stories of heartbreak and most of those stories began with their parents.

With that being said, we must remember to separate the woman from the devil within her.

Of course, some people choose to serve the devil, but then again, there are some who simply do not know how to serve God.

This book is written for men who want to avoid immoral woman or be set free from their grip. It's also written for the women who want to become Proverbs 31:10-31 women. To do this, we must understand the plans, plots and schemes of the enemy.

The Beginning

The very first people on the face of this Earth were Adam and Eve. Of course, God created Adam first, and then Eve. Now, if we look at the text throughout the Bible, we will see that God generally gave the greatest blessing to the firstborn and this practice continued on with the men of old. In biblical times, a man would oftentimes bless his oldest son and leave the greatest portion of an inheritance to him. The blessing was referred to as a "birthright" and the eldest sons would often get a double portion of it. The other sons would get blessed but they wouldn't receive as much as the first son. This is why Jacob asked Esau to sell him his birthright. This is also likely why Sarah insisted that Isaac be sent away. It wasn't mandated for a father to give his firstborn the priestly blessing, but it was tradition.

With that being said, we can now better understand one of the reasons that God gave men authority over women. Men were God's firstborn and as such, they received the judicial authority over their households. God's intention for men was that each man would manage his home the very same way that God manages the heavens and the Earth.

Genesis 1:27 tells us that we were created in the image of God. This means that God, in a sense, replicated Himself when He created us. We were created to think like Him, love like Him and be like Him. We were created to worship Him. His thoughts are higher than our thoughts and His ways are better than our ways (see Isaiah 55:8). That's the way it is supposed to be, but it goes without saying that sin perverted us. When Adam and Eve gave in to temptation, sin entered into mankind through them.

Eve was first tempted by the devil. No one

knows why Satan chose to approach Eve, but it is likely because Satan wanted to attack the order that God had established. He wanted the woman to fall first so she could then lead her husband into sin. Before sin entered mankind, there was only one rule and that was: Adam and Eve were not to eat from the Tree of the Knowledge of Good and Evil. There was no need for God to establish Adam as the head of his home because both Adam and Eve were sinless. When sin entered in, a protective order had to be established.

The story of the fall of mankind is a well-known one. Satan tempted Eve and she gave in to the temptation. She then went to her husband and gave him the very poison that she was eating. No one knows how she convinced Adam to eat the fruit or whether she had to convince him at all. The Bible simply tells us that she gave some of the fruit to Adam and he ate it. This is called seduction. To seduce means to "lead astray." Satan, through Eve, led Adam into sin.

After their fall, God then gave husbands authority over their wives.

Genesis 3:16 (NLT): Then he said to the woman, "I will sharpen the pain of your pregnancy, and in pain you will give birth. And you will desire to control your husband, but he will rule over you."

1 Corinthians 11:3 (ESV): But I want you to understand that the head of every man is Christ, the head of a wife is her husband, and the head of Christ is God.

One thing you need to know about seduction is that it is not always sexual. The average person thinks about sex when they hear the word "seduction" and that's because over the years, we've zoomed in on one area of seduction, but ignored the others. A mother can seduce her son or her daughter to commit sin. This means that she can led them astray. A son can seduce his father and a daughter can seduce her mother. The objective of the seducer is to convince the person who they are trying to seduce that whatever sin they are tempting them with will give them some favorable benefits. The core of seduction is selfish ambition, the inventor of seduction is Satan and the goal of seduction is to cause one to fall away from God in the very same manner that Satan fell away from Him.

When Satan fell from Heaven, it is largely believed that a third of heaven's angels fell with him, were cursed, and are now what we call demons (see Revelation 12:7). The question is ... how was he able to convince them to rise up against God with him? The answer is simple. He likely seduced them in the very same way that he seduced Eve. Additionally, after he seduced Eve, he didn't have to seduce Adam because Eve had given in to temptation, and therefore, would be a temptress. This means that she would tempt Adam with the very same sin she'd fallen into.

To this day, Satan loves to use seduction

because it causes others to fall into the very same trap he set for himself (lust). *Satan lusted for power and control.* Additionally, it has a domino effect, wherein people who fall into the seductive snares of the enemy will promote the sin they're in. No one wants to fall alone, so people who fall into temptation will often cause others to fall.

Sin came in and perverted us, meaning it altered God's design of us. God formed us, but sin deformed us, making us look less like God and more like the devil. That's why God tells us to be transformed by the renewing of our minds. This journey we call life is about finding our way back to the image of God; we are simply trying to find our way back to Eden. The great news is the Word of God came in the flesh (Jesus Christ) and made this all possible. Jesus Christ is referred to as the second Adam (see 1 Corinthians 15:45).

Satan understands spiritual things because he

is a spirit; a wicked one. He understands who God is, how He works and what He wants. For this reason, Satan learned to use our design against us. Once he successfully tempted Eve into eating from the Tree of the Knowledge of Good and Evil, Satan knew that sin would produce a domino effect, meaning that every child born of Adam and Eve would automatically be bound by sinful nature. Why is this? We create after our own. When God designed us, He told us to reproduce. The word "reproduce" means to repeat production, or better yet, recreate what we are. God creates; we recreate. We will always birth children created in our own likeness. So when Adam and Eve sinned against God, any child they reproduced would bear their sins and that child's children would bear his or her sins. This was the fall of mankind.

Jesus Christ came and set us free from the curse of the law and He reconciled us to the Father, Himself. Whereas, sin once exiled us from Him, the Blood of Jesus reconciled us to Him. Nevertheless, the nature of the flesh is still sin, even though our spirits are instantly changed the moment we are saved. Because of this, we still wrestle with the sinful nature and desires of our flesh. Additionally, whatever sins our parents, grandparents, great-grandparents and ancestors wrestled with becomes the strongmen that we wrestle with ... if they were not delivered from them before they became parents. This is what we commonly refer to as a generational curse.

Satan managed to get sin into the natural realm. He managed to get mankind to sin, but that wasn't enough for him. Because he understands the powerful nature of sin, he understands that sin will lead a man in all of his choices. It will determine what he does in life and it will determine who he has children with. This means it will determine who he chooses (or unintentionally causes) to bear his children. A man who is led astray by sin will find women who have been led astray by sin, and while in their sin, they will likely come together and produce children. These children will bear the sinful nature of their parents so, for example, if the father is a sexually perverted alcoholic, his sons and daughters will likely wrestle with sexual perversion and alcoholism. Even if his children won't wrestle with the same strongholds, it will be in their bloodline and will eventually manifest in his grandchildren or great-grandchildren. The same goes for the mother. Like the man, a woman is full of something; whether that something be generational godliness or generational rebellion. Whatever is in her, she will also pour into her children. So, each child born is a vessel full of what that child's parents poured into him or her. That's why we have to be reborn; God wants to empty out the old so that we don't reproduce our sinful nature.

When a man sins against God and is rebellious, he robs his son (and daughters) of a birthright because in sin, Satan will steal whatsoever a man has. When mankind sins against God, like Adam and Eve, God has to send them away from the place that he wanted to bless them in. This is why God tells us that a "good man" leaves an inheritance for his children and his children's children (see Proverbs 13:22).

We must understand that Satan is after a man's seed (his future children), just as he is after the womb of a woman. If he can control what goes into the womb, he can control what comes out of the womb. Satan wants to contaminate every man with as much sin as he can get into him, and while a man is yet in his sin, Satan will produce women for him to sin with. The goal is to entertain him in his sin so that he never seeks to leave it, and Satan's ultimate goal is to get his seed. The women who entertain men in sin are themselves in sin, and therefore, will birth out children who are slaves to the sins of their parents. Truthfully, the children would be even worse than both parents because they will bear the sins of both parents.

A seductress is a seed-seeker. Her demonic assignment is to get the seed of a man and to cause him to birth children when he is not a "good man bearing a good name". This ensures that he does not have an inheritance to leave to his children or grandchildren; plus, his name will not be blessed. Instead, his name will be forgotten or forever stained by his choices.

Proverbs 22:1 (ESV): A good name is to be chosen rather than great riches, and favor is better than silver or gold.

John 15:16 (ESV): You did not choose me, but I chose you and appointed you that you should go and bear fruit and that your fruit should abide, so that whatever you ask the Father in my name, he may give it to you.

Adam's name was ruined because of the sin he entered. Nevertheless, God changed the name of Abram to Abraham and blessed him to be the father of many nations. Why did God change Abram's name? The old name represented the old man and Abram's sin nature; the new name represented the new creature and the nature of the blessing that God was about to bestow upon Abraham (the new creation).

Satan attacked mankind in the beginning and he is always working to destroy the family unit. He has to catch a man before he is saved, sanctified and filled with the Holy Spirit so that he can extract that man's seed from him. At the same time, a man who is saved, sanctified and filled with the Holy Spirit is also on his menu because if he births children while in rebellion, his children will be born into several strongholds, including a spirit called religiousness. This spirit is the one behind what the Bible describes as "having a form of godliness, but denying the power thereof" (see 2 Timothy 3:5).

An immoral woman is not just a weapon formed against a man; she is a weapon formed against that man's lineage and his name. I believe this book will help both men and women understand the role and power of a seductress. It will help women to understand why Satan tries to tempt them into tempting men. Once we understand the assignment and plans of the enemy, we can go about life with a godly perspective ... one that will help us see the spirit behind everything and every person, rather than focusing on what we see in the natural.

The Faces of Seduction

God uses the natural to explain the supernatural. What we see happening in the natural realm is oftentimes just God ministering to us about the realm of the spirit. One example is a practice in the insect world called "sexual cannibalism."

In sexual cannibalism, the female insect mates with the male and then proceeds to kill him after (or during) the mating ritual. One such insect is the female praying mantis. She lures males with pheromones and when one comes along, he dances to win her favor. If she likes his dance moves, she will let him mate with her. During and sometimes after the mating commences, she will proceed to eat him alive, starting with his head. The head represents authority.

Another insect who has a reputation for eating her lover is the black widow spider, hence her name. A male will carefully approach the female in her web and he will start moving around and touching her gently. Scientists believe he does this so that she won't think he's food that's gotten caught in her web, especially since he's a lot smaller than her. If she allows him to approach her, he will then begin mating with her. After the mating is finished, most male widow spiders are able to escape alive, but some are not so fortunate. Of course, this is limited to a certain class of black widow spiders and some scientists believe that some of the male spiders offer themselves as living sacrifices in order to increase fertilization in the female.

This is what an immoral woman does. Even though she does not cannibalize her mate, she prepares him to be devoured by the enemy. To Satan, the Earth is a big lake and men are but fish in that lake. A man's anointing and influence are both representatives of how big of a fish he is in Satan's eyes. A good woman is a crown to her husband; she is favor manifested in the flesh. Howbeit, an immoral woman is bait that Satan uses. He will use her to fish for men. She may be anointed herself, but in Satan's eyes, she may be small fish designed to help him catch an even bigger fish. If the woman is big fish—meaning she's anointed to do many things—Satan will use her to fish for even bigger fish. He wants her to prey on the lives of her lovers.

Proverbs 6:26 (KJV): For by means of a whorish woman a man is brought to a piece of bread: and the adulteress will hunt for the precious life.

The word "seductress" is synonymous with the words adulteress, temptress, enchantress and sorceress. When we look at these words, we can better understand each of her functions.

The Seductress

To seduce means to "lead astray." One of the key words in this is "lead." A husband is designed to be the head of his home; this is biblical, however, the seductress has to take the lead in order to fully entrap a man. This doesn't mean that she'll walk around making demands. Instead, she will likely use demonic devices such as manipulation, witchcraft and charm to lead her prey away from sound-reasoning. When an immoral woman is demonically led to act as the seductress, her assignment is to get the guy to walk away from the path he's on. She needs to get him to follow her and she'll oftentimes do this by distracting him with her body and charming him with her words.

The Adulteress

The power of the adulteress is to divide and subtract. God adds blessings to us; He adds a wife to her husband, and then, He continues to add to the couple. He gives them children and blessings. He is a God of increase. Nevertheless, Satan is a devourer. His goal is to take away from the people he's using; therefore, he uses the adulteress to divide homes. When this is done, he can effectively subtract the blessings of God from a man.

The adulteress doesn't just attack established marriages. Her assignment is to keep godly marriages from ever happening. She does this by getting romantically involved with any and every man who Satan assigns her to.

The Temptress

Of course, we see that the word "temptress" is tied to the word "temptation." When the immoral woman yields the power of the temptress, she will use her body to tempt the man she has seduced into sin. She may do this by kissing him passionately or by luring him to her house.

When she yields the power of the temptress,

her goal isn't just to tempt the man; it is to lure him further into temptation and to cause him to give in to that temptation. She will likely do this by having sexual contact with him.

The Enchantress and the Sorceress

The seductress, adulteress and temptress may sound "attractive" to a man who's been seduced by Hollywood's favorable depiction of such a woman. Nevertheless, she is far from beautiful in God's eyes. What lurks in her is a hideous beast with the appetite of hell. Its desire is to devour the men who unwittingly place themselves at her mercy.

She is an enchantress and a sorceress ... in short, she is a witch; whether we want to acknowledge that or not.

Note: The word "enchant" means "to put under a spell." Other synonyms include: captivate, hypnotize, entrance, mesmerize, bewitch, charm, etc.

Spells are almost always performed with words. Just like God created everything with words, the enemy tries to mimic Him. He likes to use man's ability to speak life and death to his own advantage. So, for the enchantress, Satan teaches her to speak into the atmosphere whatever it is that she wants. If the man is single and she wants to marry him, the enchantress will repeatedly release her wishes into the air. (Satan is the prince of the powers of the air.) If the man is married and the enchantress wants to take him from his wife, she will release the spirits behind divorce with her tongue and she will speak all manners of evil over the relationship. If the enchantress wants her lover's money, she will release her wishes into the air. She may tell her friends or family members, but either way, Satan will use her tongue to speak curses over that man, his family, his finances and whatever it is that she wants.

After the words are released, Satan will teach

the enchantress to escalate her witchcraft. She will begin manipulating her prey using sex, emotions, his feelings for her, or his fear of losing something. She may even intentionally become pregnant to give herself some extra leverage. This is the unleashing of the sorceress, or better yet, the witch. Truthfully, some of the words we use are designed to glamorize an ungodly behavior. We must call things as they are; that way, people will seek to get set free. *When I was a seductress, if someone had told me that I was operating as a witch and the spell-binding power I was using was sensuality, sex, manipulation and words, I would have taken a second look at my choices. Like most seductresses, I tried to glamorize my behaviors and this made it easier for me to continue in them.*

An immoral woman doesn't always look like an immoral woman. As a matter of fact, one of the beliefs I picked up while in the world (and I still believe to this day) is that some of the most immoral women look "normal." Most of my friends were immoral, but the most immoral ones were the ones who wore baggy clothes, danced like men and mocked super feminine women. You can't always tell how promiscuous a woman is just by looking at her or talking with her. Some women are open and honest about who and what they are, while others have to be discerned.

Understanding Her Powers

I was 20 or 21 years old when I took a friend of
mine to her first male-exotic extravaganza
(strip show). I lived in a city in Mississippi
where entertainers rarely visited, but anytime I
heard that a strip show was coming to town, I
would rush to buy tickets. I would also call my
friends so that they could hurry and get their
tickets. Normally, we would all go together, but
on this particular night, none of my regular
hang-out buddies could come. Instead, I found
another friend who'd never been to one of
these events and invited her out with me.

We arrived at the club early and found a seat
near the main aisle ... the aisle I knew the
dancers would be walking down as they
seduced the women. We sat down and talked
as the building filled with women who were like
ourselves: lust-filled, immoral and bound by

ungodly imaginations. The music began to play, but the show still hadn't started. This was the norm. The entertainers were still fully dressed. There were about six or seven of them and they were standing near the bar, talking with one another. Since this was going to be my friend's first time seeing live exotic dancers, I wanted her to have a great time.

"Do you want the strippers to keep coming to our table tonight?" I asked.

Michelle was curious. "How are you going to do that?" she countered inquisitively.

"I can get them over here if you want. Do you want our table to be the hot spot tonight?" I asked again trying to speak over the music.

Michelle smiled and nodded her head in affirmation.

"What are you going to do?"

"What do you want to drink?"

"What's good here? Wait. Tiffany, what are you up to?"

"Their strawberry daiquiris are good. Do you want one of those?"

"Sure, but you didn't answer the question.
What are you up to?"
"Okay, I'll be back."

My confidence was at an all-time high; it was
nothing short of demonic. I rose from my seat
and walked over to the bar. "Two strawberry
daiquiris," I said, all the while, completely
ignoring the men who had suddenly stopped
talking to stare at me. While the bartender
was making my drinks, I looked in the direction
of the men, but I didn't say a word. I then
turned around and looked in the direction of my
friend. Once the bartender gave me my drinks,
I walked back to my seat and placed Michelle's
drink in front of her.
"Okay, every last one of them will be at our
table tonight," I said.
Michelle was perplexed. "What did you do? I
didn't see you say anything to them."
I couldn't explain it; I just knew that I'd set a trap
and they would fall into it.

I wasn't a curvaceous woman and I definitely wasn't the prettiest woman there. If you had asked me, I saw myself as an average woman, but somehow, I knew that as a woman, I possessed a certain power. I also knew that men who are accustomed to getting a lot of attention almost always chase the women who ignore them. Of course, I was scantily clad, wearing a red midriff shirt and a mini skirt, but compared to some of the women there, I was well-covered. Nevertheless, the revealing clothing would not be enough to capture their attention; my over-the-top confidence and demonic knowledge of men was my lure. I was nothing but Devil Bait.

Sure enough, our table was the "hot spot" that night. Every dancer made his way to our table and pulled me out of my seat when it was his turn to dance. Finally, when the dancer who was considered the main attraction was about to come out, a few of the other guys came and got the aisle ready for him. They placed a single chair in the center of the aisle, and then one of the men came over to me and said that the dancer had requested that I be sat in that chair. Michelle was having the time of her life. She kept asking me excitedly, "What did you do?!"

I couldn't really answer her. I had simply learned to master sensuality. Believe it or not, I'd unknowingly tapped into what the Bible refers to as a "power."

Ephesians 6:12 (KJV): For we wrestle not against flesh and blood, but against principalities, against powers, against the rulers of the darkness of this world, against spiritual wickedness in high places.

Those strippers were not guarded, so I didn't hesitate to question whether I could seduce them or not. I knew that I could. *I would have been severely humbled if I hadn't.* But the truth is that many men of God do not realize the power that an immoral woman possesses. She can size up a man's anointing and if he is not guarded by holiness, she will confidently say in her heart or out loud that she can have him. The worst part is … she is not lying.

During that period in my life, I unknowingly tapped into the power of sensuality. Sensuality has everything to do with the five senses: sight (this is the lure), hearing (words are the bait), touch (the softness of an immoral woman's hands can cause a man to fall under her spell), smell (an immoral woman releases a scent that attracts unguarded men) and taste (when a man kisses her, he tastes her essence and is immediately trapped by her).

Sensuality functions by appealing to a man's fantasies. These are the imaginations that the Bible told him to cast down, but he did not. **2 Corinthians 10:5 (KJV):** Casting down imaginations, and every high thing that exalteth itself against the knowledge of God, and bringing into captivity every thought to the obedience of Christ.

When a man does not cast down ungodly imaginations, lust will eventually capture him and it will have to be cast out of him. Basically, he has a choice. He can bring his thoughts into captivity or they will capture and enslave him. Anything that is not cast down makes its way into his heart and begins to influence his thoughts and decisions.

Proverbs 4:23 (NIV): Above all else, guard your heart, for everything you do flows from it.

To understand the powers of an immoral woman, you must first understand what "powers" are. Ephesians 6:12 tells us that we wrestle against the following:

- principalities
- powers
- rulers of the darkness of this world
- spiritual wickedness in high places

Principality: A principality is a chief demon. The word "principality" comes from the word "prince"; meaning that the demon in question is a ruler or head authority. It is also known as the "principle demon." An example of a principality is Beelzebub, who the Bible refers to as "the prince of devils" (see Luke 11:15). Another example is the Prince of Persia (see Daniel 10:13).

Principalities rule over regions, groups and families. You will always know what principality is in operation when you notice a common sin or stronghold in a region, neighborhood or family. For example, in certain cities, states and countries, you will notice a lot of scantily clad women walking about. If you check the numbers, more than likely you'll notice that that particular place has a higher rate of sexually transmitted diseases, divorce and the like. Of course, there will be more children born into single-parent households, which means that there will be more poverty. In this region, the Baal principality will likely be in operation and will release the following demonic spirits: Jezebel, Ahab, Athaliah, poverty, fornication, adultery, abandonment, idolatry, lust, divorce, pride, etc.

Powers: Powers are legalized authorities (demons) that have been allowed by mankind. Whatever we bind on earth is bound in Heaven and whatever we loose on earth is loosed in Heaven (see Matthew 18:18).

Mankind has the ability to loose things because God gave us dominion over the earth. However, in addition to loosing things, believers in specific, also have the ability to bind things. This power is godly and was given to us through Christ Jesus. Anytime a demonic power is prevalent, it is because the church in that region has failed to use their ability to bind and loose. When an immoral woman uses her powers on a man, she is using whatever legal authority the kingdom of darkness has over him through his sin.

In deliverance ministry, I've noticed that some

demons will speak out when the deliverance minister tries to cast them out. They'll say things like, "I'm not leaving! I have a legal right to be here, so you cannot make me leave!" I've had demons say these things to me when attempting to help deliver someone from demonic oppression. Each time that happened, I commanded the demons to tell me what legal right (power) they had to that person. The demons would oftentimes be reluctant to give up this information, but when commanded to release that information (in Jesus's name), they told me what rights they felt they had. Oftentimes, it was unforgiveness in the person that had given the demons the right to inhabit that person. In some cases, the demons claimed to have gained rights through the sins of that person's ancestors. The point is ... the person is bound because he or she did not use the legal authority given to him or her by God to bind the demons. Their sins and fears had given the demons the legal right to inhabit them.

Rulers of the Darkness of This World: These are world rulers or influential people. There are demon princes (principalities) and then there are human princes and princesses who operate as rulers on Earth.

Rulers don't necessarily have to be kings or queens to rule. They simply need to carry a great influence over people. Of course, they are headed up by the principalities who use them to promote sin, the occult and demonic doctrines.

Examples of rulers of darkness include, but are not limited to: Catholic priests, leaders of anti-Christ religions, many (if not most) of today's celebrities and even some leaders in Christian churches. We must remember that not everyone who says, "Lord, Lord" will enter Heaven (see Matthew 7:21).

Spiritual Wickedness in High Places: In some translations, this phrase is written as "spiritual wickedness in heavenly places." The Bible tells us that God made mankind a little lower than angels. What exactly does this mean? Angels are referred to as the "sons of God" and we have now been adopted as sons and daughters of God through Christ Jesus. Satan and every demonic force has fallen; they are the lowest life forms in existence; nevertheless, they desire to regain their previous positions. Satan wants to take God's place, but he's been judged and there is no salvation available for him. For this reason, demons must "borrow" authority from believers. Demons are trying to climb back to the top, using human beings as their step stools. Demons want to gain as much authority as possible so they will use unbelievers and backslidden believers to get to the new believers. New believers, in most cases, haven't entirely separated themselves from sin yet, so they are easily accessible to the enemy.

Satan will then use the new believers to gain

access to seasoned believers who are not satisfied with their lives or churches. That's how they convince seasoned believers that they need to embrace worldly styles of music and dance to grow their churches. Demons will monitor seasoned believers and try to find ways to infiltrate their lives. After they gain access to seasoned, mature believers, they will try to go after godly leaders because a godly leader, to them, is a "high place." If a demon can cause a leader to backslide or rebel against God, that demon will cause the leader to operate very similar to a principality. The leader is a ruler over the people he or she is leading, so he or she is always making impartations. Demons want to contaminate a man or woman of God so that they can become "rulers" and operate over the group that the Christian leader is leading. This is also true for governmental offices or any seat of authority in the world.

To understand the "powers" of an immoral

woman, you must first understand that her powers are demonic. When she approaches a man or is approached by a man, the demons who are operating in and through her will seek to find some legal ground to access and attack that man. Chances are, if men approach her, they do so because they are led astray by lust. This is enough to give her demons access to them, but a demon's strength in a man is fully dependent on how far in sin that man is, so devils want more than just lustful stares. They want a bridge between that man and the woman he's lusting after, so they need her to create a soul-tie with him. If a soul-tie is created, demons will gain access to the man and everyone he's been given authority over (his wife, children, church, etc.). Nevertheless, the access they have is still limited to the sin he's in and the depth of that sin. They need him to go deeper and deeper into sin so that they can increase their kingdom within him by causing him to give his strength (authority) away.

Proverbs 31:3 (ESV): Do not give your strength to women, your ways to those who destroy kings.

To gain greater access to him, demons will cause him to despise his wife ... if he's married, for example. By despising his wife, he will begin to mistreat her and this may open her up to demonic oppression. She'll likely be hurt, angry and confused. She won't be able to concentrate on whatever it is that God wants her to focus on. In her anger, she may open herself up for the enemy to gain greater access to her children. The goal of these demons is to get the family so far away from God that it is almost impossible for them to return to Him. All of this can be set in motion by an immoral woman whose powers are not bound, but are allowed to operate against a family.

When dealing with the adulteress, what many don't know is that her assignment is to solely destroy that marriage. She doesn't know that;

she just sees something she wants and she'll go after it at any cost. Nevertheless, the mistake is in thinking that she wants the man. This is not always the truth. In most cases, she is a broken woman who has learned to compete against other women, so her real prize is in winning. If she can destroy that marriage and get that man's wife to give herself to someone else, her feelings for the guy and about the relationship will change drastically. I've actually seen this many times. Many adulteresses think they want the men they are having affairs with, but they don't. They are broken souls who see competition as a beauty pageant.

I've witnessed adulteresses "win" the guys they were seeing and hold on to them just long enough for their divorces to be finalized and their wives to remarry. After that, they had an epiphany. They suddenly discovered that they did not want the men they'd fought so hard to get. Some of them even realized that they despised the men. Nevertheless, adulteresses can often be heard saying things like, "I don't care who he's with. I just don't want him to reconcile with his wife." For her, it was all about winning against the wife; that's it and that's all. If the husband and wife were to reconcile, their reconciliation, to her, represents her being defeated.

To "win" the men the adulteresses are seeing, they often use a power called "charm." If you have ever seen a snake being charmed, you will notice that it follows the movement of the man who's charming it. It gives off the appearance that it is hypnotized or dancing to the music, but in truth, snakes do not have ears. They are deaf, so they rely on their sight when being charmed. The charmer tries to remain at a safe distance and the snakes are oftentimes sluggish, making it hard for them to attack the charmer. This is how charm works.

When a woman charms a man, she uses her

words to "deafen" him to the sound of the Word of God and anything that can help set him free. She wants him to rely on his eyesight; that way, she can physically seduce him with her beauty, all the while distracting him with her body and movements. This is called "bewitching" and is a well-disguised witchcraft. This is why the word "seductress" is synonymous with the words "sorceress" and "enchantress."

Proverbs 31:30 (ESV): Charm is deceitful, and beauty is vain, but a woman who fears the LORD is to be praised.

Galatians 3:1 (KJV): O foolish Galatians, who hath bewitched you, that ye should not obey the truth, before whose eyes Jesus Christ hath been evidently set forth, crucified among you?

Other powers that men have to be aware of lie in the woman's body. Some women employ demonic powers through their eyes, breasts, legs, thighs, buttocks and lips. For example, there is a demonic gaze that some immoral women use to capture their lovers. I've even seen seductive women in ministry use this gaze. I'm familiar with it because I was a seductress; plus, I was surrounded by seductresses. Believe it or not, immoral women do know the power of their eyes and they will use their eyes to bind men. This means they imprison them in a place that we often call, "falling in love." Biblically speaking, this is not a place that has been established by God. It is a place of heightened passion, lust, lasciviousness and captivation. Understand this: to be captivated means to be captured. **Proverbs 6:25 (NASB):** Do not desire her beauty in your heart, nor let her capture you with her eyelids.

Some would argue that it is not ungodly to "fall in love," but in truth, God is love. We fall into sin, but when we repent, we intentionally get back up again. So, what is it then that we should be experiencing? It's simple: love without the fall. When people fall, they fall into temptation and they fall into the snares of the enemy. We can love people and experience the heightened emotions we experienced when we "fell in love" with others in the past, but true love does not lead to a fall; sin does.

When a woman has powers in her breasts, she will wear clothing that brings attention to her cleavage. Men who are led astray by their lusts will look into her cleavage and become "captivated" or better yet, "captured." When her powers are in her legs, men will find themselves enticed by the way she walks. Again, this is how many men become captives of the demons in immoral women.

Proverbs 5:20 (NLT): Why be captivated, my son, by an immoral woman, or fondle the breasts of a promiscuous woman?

When you play a video of a sexually immoral woman, pay attention to her behaviors. They have powers in their eyes and will often stare seductively into the camera before speaking.

(Yes, this includes some women in ministry! I've seen it.) They may act as if they don't know the camera is on for a few seconds and they will use that time to set their demonic traps. Men who are entranced by her seductive gaze will find themselves saying things to her like, "You're sexy" or "You'd better stop looking like that before you get me in trouble." What is in them is identifying with what is in her. It's basically saying, "I see you."

I remember when I moved to Germany in 2009. I was delivered, for the most part, from many of the demons I once had, but my deliverance was not yet complete. I'd taken a picture earlier that year and posted it on Facebook. It wasn't an illicit photo, of course; it was what I felt was a normal photo of me looking into the camera. I was married then, but marriage does not deliver people from demons.

I'd started designing Myspace pages and websites and a man reached out to me and asked that I do some work for him. He claimed his ministry was centered around sex, or dealing with the issues centered around sex. He would call me often and I found myself being really mean to him because I kept noticing how he was trying to passively pry into my life and marriage. I recognized the spirit that was operating in him.

One day, he saw the photo that I'd shared on Facebook. He called me under the guise of wanting to ask questions about some graphics he wanted to have designed, but in truth, he'd seen something in me that he wanted to connect with. After asking me about pricing, he said, "I want to be your friend." I asked him what he meant, and he said, "I want to be your special friend." Of course, I questioned (and rebuked) him, but he went on to say, "I saw the picture you posted and I can see it in your eyes." I didn't know what he meant by "it," but what I did know was that whatever "it" was, I didn't want it. I ended all dealings with him, but it was at that moment that I realized that men were still approaching me in an ungodly way. I then began to seek the Lord about setting me free from anything that offended Him.

I was fully clothed on that picture, but the gaze I gave on that photo was nothing but the equivalent of a demon posing for a photo. I needed deliverance, but I didn't know it because I was married, faithful, and most of all, loving the Lord. Nevertheless, what was in me had been in me long before I'd gotten married. The closer I got to God, the more I was able to see the darkness that I needed to be delivered from.

When sexually immoral women have demonic powers in their tongues or lips, they will often speak seductively or move their lips in a seductive way. Again, this includes some women in ministry. If you ever want to see if a woman in ministry has a spirit of seduction and is using her powers to ensnare men, watch

one of her videos and hit mute. That way,
you're not distracted by what she's saying, but
you will see the seductive manner in which she
forms her words. The goal of this is to draw
men in and "captivate" them. Understand that
there are some God-fearing women in ministry
who need deliverance from the spirit of
seduction. Some of them are even married
(marriage does not set one free from demonic
spirits). Satan has convinced them that they are
simply different and anyone who questions
their seductive mannerisms is jealous of them,
but this is all a lie. Satan's objective is to
ensure that they don't seek to be free. After
all, he wants them to sit in the pulpit and
capture the men who approach them for
prayer.

When a demon is influencing a sexually immoral
woman to use her buttocks to "captivate" men,
the woman will oftentimes insist on walking in
front of the men she is trying to capture. She
will wear fitted-clothing and be (intentionally)

clumsy. Instead of squatting to pick up whatever it is that she has dropped (squatting is actually more comfortable), an immoral woman will bend over with her butt raised in the air. When you see a woman like this, she is being used as Devil Bait. She has set her trap and is trying to lure unsuspecting men into it. Many of these women will wear fitted dresses to church and insist on sitting near the front of the church. They will stand up more than most people and dance around every time the music plays. They may even need more bathroom breaks than others. Again, this is the seductress hunting for her prey. The church, to her, is her camouflage and her dress is the lure. That's how immoral women entrap immoral men.

If lust is found in a man, he will fall into one of the traps of the enemy; after all, Satan has many traps and they come in various sizes and colors. A seductive woman's power is only relevant when it comes in contact with a man

who is not guarded by holiness. Once a man
presents his body as a living sacrifice, holy and
acceptable to God, the seductress will be
rendered powerless against him.

Sex in the Bible

In every generation, a woman who has had multiple sex partners outside the covenant of marriage has been labeled and ostracized by society. The reason for this is that society has always drawn its strength from following a set of rules designed to keep evil out and promote good. The strength of a society was and still is in the laws it carries and its ability to enforce those laws. Amazingly enough, this is even true for many pagan or godless societies. People have always understood the need for rules and laws because a lawless society is always going to be a place that's overrun and overcome by evil.

Promiscuity is a practice that has been shunned in many societies, cultures and religions, including some pagan religions. At the same time, some cultures and religions promote it,

especially male promiscuity. This is because
many believe that a man's strength and power
lies in the number of wives he has, the number
of women he has slept with, the number of
women he has romantic access to, and the
number of children he has. In Biblical times,
most men who had multiple wives were rich,
powerful men and this helped to establish the
belief that women and children were the
epitome of wealth. This practice wasn't
shunned in the Old Testament biblical days if:

- the sex occurred between a man and a
  virgin.
- the man had the permission of the
  virgin's father to "wed" her.
- the man could provide for his many
  wives and the children that were born to
  him through them.
- the man kept and provided for his new
  bride for the rest of her life (divorcing
  her could be a dishonor to her father's
  house and name).

As long as these rules were followed, a Jewish

man could have as many wives as he could financially, morally and physically handle. If a man had intercourse with a woman without her father's permission (the equivalent of premarital sex in those days), and he did not take her out of her father's house, the woman in question would be considered immoral and her father's house could be written off as lawless and immoral. At the same time, a man's daughter was considered more of a responsibility than a legal heir because the males carried on their fathers' names. A woman, on the other hand, would eventually carry on the name of her husband's forefathers and she would raise up children that bore his name. In other words, she would become a part of an external lineage, representing her husband and his family and not-so-much her biological father. For this reason, women, although equally loved by their fathers, would be seen as property. Truthfully, in those times, their reasoning was different than the reasoning of our generation. If we'd called a woman the property of her father back then, we would have insulted not only the father, but the daughter because fathers loved both their daughters and their sons. Nevertheless, because of tradition, a man's goal was to carry on his name. So, most Jewish men would raise up moral, law-abiding daughters who would, as we would say these days, make their fathers look good to general society. They were tokens of their father's wealth and integrity. If a man had beautiful, sane virgins for daughters, he would be considered a man of good standing and his household was considered blessed.

In the Biblical days, Jewish women did not walk around with their faces covered, contrary to popular belief. Much like the men, they wore headdresses, but the only time they wore veils was when they were being introduced to the men they were to marry. Prostitutes covered their faces to hide their identities. This means that many of Hollywood's depictions of the women in the Bible are false and misleading.

One of the Bible's stories involves a woman named Tamar and her father in law, Judah. Tamar was married to Judah's son, Er, but because of Er's wickedness, the Bible says that the Lord put him to death. As with Jewish custom, Judah then told his other son, Onan, to go and "raise offspring for his brother." In those times, such a practice meant that the brother of the deceased man would take the deceased man's wife as his own wife, but the firstborn son that he had with her would not be considered his son; he would be considered the son of the deceased man. This meant that the child in question would receive the deceased man's inheritance and would carry on his name. This was called a Levirate marriage. Levirate marriages were established as a part of Old Testament Law and was described in Deuteronomy 25.

Deuteronomy 25:5-10 (ESV): If brothers dwell together, and one of them dies and has no son, the wife of the dead man shall not be married outside the family to a stranger. Her husband's brother shall go in to her and take her as his wife and perform the duty of a husband's brother to her. And the first son whom she bears shall succeed to the name of his dead brother, that his name may not be blotted out of Israel. And if the man does not wish to take his brother's wife, then his brother's wife shall go up to the gate to the elders and say, "My husband's brother refuses to perpetuate his brother's name in Israel; he will not perform the duty of a husband's brother to me." Then the elders of his city shall call him and speak to him, and if he persists, saying, "I do not wish to take her," then his brother's wife shall go up to him in the presence of the elders and pull his sandal off his foot and spit in his face. And she shall answer and say, "So shall it be done to the man who does not build up his brother's house." And the name of his house shall be called in Israel, "The house of him who had his sandal pulled off."

Onan didn't want to have children for his

brother, Er, so the Bible recounts his wicked deed. He had sex with Tamar, meaning, he took her on as his wife, but he chose to use one of the most used and least effective methods of birth control ... a method that is still practiced to this day: the withdrawal method. The Bible says that Onan spilled his semen on the ground and this act was displeasing to God, so God put him to death.

Judah had another son left by the name of Shelah, but he was underage, so Judah told Tamar to return to her father's house temporarily. He said that when Shelah was of age, he would send Shelah to marry her. Tamar was considered the property of Judah's family and could not marry anyone else. Here we have two people who have been affected by the loss of their loved ones, but both people had different perspectives. More than likely, Judah believed that Tamar was an accursed woman because the two sons who'd married her ended up dead. Tamar, on the other hand,

likely saw this as an unfortunate turn of events
that had nothing to do with her, so she wanted
to move forward with Jewish customs; she
wanted to marry Shelah, Judah's youngest son.
Because of their different perspectives, both
people deceived each other to get what they
wanted. Judah tried to break the Levirate
marriage law by sending Tamar to her father's
house. He had no intentions of sending Shelah
to get Tamar; after all, he could have allowed
Tamar to stay in his house. He chose to send
her to her father's house because he wanted
to rid himself of what he believed to be an
accursed woman. Tamar decided to address
her father-in-law's deception in a very public
manner.

We must understand that the women in those
days were very much like the women of today.
Many of them wanted to be married and to
have children; plus, they wanted to bring honor
to their fathers' houses. Tamar was no
different, so when Judah didn't honor his

promise to her, Tamar decided to take matters into her own hands. The Bible tells us that Tamar took off her widow's garments and she covered her face with a veil. She'd heard that Judah was going to be traveling to Timnah, so she sat at the entrance of a place called Enaim because she knew that Judah would have to pass through Enaim to get to Timnah. She wanted to seduce her father-in-law, so she covered herself in what was considered the garments of a prostitute. The Bible recounts what happened next.

Genesis 38:13-19 (ESV): And when Tamar was told, "Your father-in-law is going up to Timnah to shear his sheep," she took off her widow's garments and covered herself with a veil, wrapping herself up, and sat at the entrance to Enaim, which is on the road to Timnah. For she saw that Shelah was grown up, and she had not been given to him in marriage. When Judah saw her, he thought she was a prostitute, for she had covered her face. He turned to her at the roadside and said, "Come, let me come in to you," for he did not know that she was his daughter-in-law. She said, "What will you give me, that you may come in to me?" He answered, "I will send you a young goat from the flock." And she said, "If you give me a pledge, until you send it—" He said, "What pledge shall I give you?" She replied, "Your signet and your cord and your staff that is in your hand." So he gave them to her and went in to her, and she conceived by him. Then she arose and went away, and taking off her veil she put on the garments of her widowhood.

As we can see, there were garments of widowhood and garments considered to be those worn by prostitutes. Why did Tamar sleep with her father-in-law? She did that to honor Jewish customs and raise up children to her deceased husband and, at the same time, had she not deceived Judah, she would have likely died a childless widow in her father's house. She was considered the wife or, according to our culture, property of Judah's household and she wanted what she felt was rightfully hers. Because of this, when Judah's wife died, she took it upon herself to become his wife since he did not give his son, Shelah, to her.

The Bible tells us that Tamar became pregnant and when Judah heard that she was pregnant, he wanted to have her killed. This was largely due to the fact that she'd brought dishonor to his name; translated in modern terms, she'd publicly embarrassed him. Judah acted swiftly to regain his family's honor and ordered that Tamar be burned to death. At that time, he had the right to kill her if she'd played the harlot because she was considered his property. Nevertheless, Tamar had anticipated Judah's reaction and this is why she'd taken some of his personal property in exchange for sex with him. So, to justify herself and save her own life, Tamar sent Judah's property back to him through a mediator, stating that the father of her children was the man to whom the items belonged. Of course, Judah recognized his property and realized that Tamar had been the woman on the side of the road, the woman he'd slept with. She'd publicly addressed his private sin against her. Because of this, he said that she was more righteous than him, and according to the Bible, he never slept with her again.

Of course, Tamar used a deceptive tactic, but she did that to force Judah to honor his word. It would have been even more embarrassing to Judah's household if it had become public knowledge that he'd slept with a prostitute, impregnated her and discovered that she'd been the daughter-in-law in whom he'd deceived. In those days, many of the women who turned to prostitution had done so because they were no longer under the protection and provision of a husband or father. The women in question were oftentimes widows who could not go back to their fathers' houses or women who'd been disowned by

their fathers because they'd had sex outside of
the traditional marital covenant. Tamar's choice
to prostitute herself could have been seen by
the public as Judah's negligence to protect and
provide for the wife of his deceased son, and
his rebellion against Jewish laws. Because of
this, it did not serve Judah to have Tamar killed.
At the same time, if it had ever been said that
Tamar was a shrine prostitute, it could only
mean that Judah had gone to a pagan temple
and engaged in sex with one of the women
there. This would have brought even more
dishonor to Judah's name. Judah publicly
regarded his sin towards Tamar, thus retaining
the honor of his own name and thereby
acknowledging that she was not a prostitute;
she was simply a woman scorned.

After this, there is no mention of Judah's
relationship with Tamar, but it is recorded that
Tamar gave birth to two sons: Perez and
Zedah.

God designed sex to represent the coming

together of two people as one (in marriage). Additionally, sex was created for procreation. To encourage procreation and unity, God made sex an enjoyable experience. Nevertheless, sin entered in and man perverted the use of sex. Because of this, laws had to be created to keep the land from being defiled; meaning, God knew that sex outside of covenant would unleash a series of events that had the ability to swallow mankind as a whole. In other words, the laws created by God treated sex like a controlled substance, only to be enjoyed by those who had the prescription of marriage. The reason for this is sex is far more powerful than most people realize. It's not just a one-time event between two people. Sex establishes and strengthens soul ties, and anytime sex occurs outside the godly covenant of marriage, it occurs outside the will and the protective covering of God. This means that mankind has taken a God-instituted event and removed God from it; thus perverting it.

There were two types of prostitutes mentioned in the Bible. First, there were the prostitutes who had sex in exchange for money. Many of the women who did this did so because they were widowed or they'd been ousted from their fathers' homes and shunned by society. For example, a woman who'd been raped could be shunned by her father's household if she did not scream for help while she was being sexually assaulted. The reason for this is it could be argued by the perpetrator that the sex was consensual. Without any witnesses, such a claim could not be validated or debunked.

The second type of prostitute was a shrine or temple prostitute. Temple prostitutes used sex to honor their gods. They would have sex with the men who came to worship these deities because it was commonly believed that most of their gods and goddesses made the land fertile. It is clear that Tamar did not pose as a shrine prostitute, since the Bible does not mention a shrine when detailing Judah's encounter with her. Instead, Judah found her on the side of the road, possibly leading to a temple. This means that it is likely that he did not know what type of prostitute he was engaging with; nevertheless, he intentionally engaged in sexual misconduct with what he believed to be a prostitute. If she had been discovered to be a temple prostitute, Judah could have been found in violation of Jewish law.

The Broken Altar

Have you ever went fishing and had a fish to bite your line, only for it to get away? If so, do you remember the disappointment you felt? You likely asked yourself, "Why didn't I reel it in when I had the chance?" In most cases, it was because you didn't realize that you had a fish on the line until it was too late.

Almost every woman who has ever been romantically involved with a man has likely experienced that one guy she believed got away from her. That particular guy has had and will continue to have the greatest impact on all of her relationships until she gets saved, sanctified and filled with the Holy Spirit. Additionally, God will have to give her a new heart and a new mind, otherwise she will continue to reason, think and make decisions using the heart that was filled with wrong beliefs and then broken. Until that guy is out of her system, she won't know how to be a good woman for any man, even though she will think that she is good enough as she is. It doesn't matter how he left; what does matter is that when he got away, he took a piece of her with him and he left her broken. Additionally, he doesn't have to be the first man she's ever kissed, had sex with or called her boyfriend; he just needs to be the one who's had the greatest impact on her emotionally. He was the one who went the furthest in her heart; so, consequentially, he was the one who did the most damage to her heart.

Every man who enters a woman's life has the ability to only go a certain distance into her heart, and how far he goes will depend on:

1. How much of her heart is available.
2. Her belief system.
3. The condition of her heart.
4. Her past experiences.
5. How much she can relate to the guy.

6. Whether she believes that guy's words or not.

7. Her intentions for that guy.

How Much of Her Heart is Available

The truth is ... a person cannot give you what they've given to someone else. Sometimes, a woman's heart can be portioned out to her former lovers through regret, unforgiveness and hopes for reconciliation. If she doesn't believe that reconciliation will take place or if her former lover is with someone else, she may entertain other relationships in hopes of getting married. She may meet a new guy, give him what's left of her heart, marry the guy and have children with him, but he will always know that he doesn't have all of her. His heart will search for the missing piece of her, and all too often, he will do this by questioning her about past relationships. This will help him to key in on that one guy who still holds a piece of his wife.

Her Belief System

Some women don't believe in God. Some women don't trust God. Some women were taught that all men cheat. Some women don't believe that it's possible for a man to love them. A woman's belief system will create a wall in her heart that her lovers will find difficult to get past. The wall may allow some men to go far into her heart, while others won't be able to get past a few telephone conversations and a date. If a man does get past that wall, she will likely become obsessed with him and make an idol out of him if her heart isn't right with God.

The Condition of Her Heart

If a woman's heart is broken, a man cannot venture too far off into it without getting cut. Additionally, how far a man goes will depend on how deep her wounds are. A woman will oftentimes respond negatively when a man ventures off into the areas of her heart that she's deemed off limits.

Her Past Experiences

A woman who's suffered through a lot will have more walls and shorter stay-times in her heart than a woman who hasn't suffered much. This is, of course, if she has not healed from her past experiences.

How Much She Can Relate to the Guy

How can two walk together except they be agreed? This is scriptural (see Amos 3:3). The key word is "together." It is possible for two people to be in a relationship who cannot relate to one another, however, they won't be able to "walk together;" meaning that they won't go far as a couple. When a woman can relate to a man, in most cases, she will open up more of her heart to him than she has with her former lovers. That's why it's dangerous for a husband to close himself off emotionally from his wife, and then tolerate his wife having male friends in whom she confides in. This behavior allows the male friends more access to her heart and the results will start to reflect in their marriage.

Whether She Believes the Guy's Words or Not

Let's face it ... if a woman doesn't believe the words that her boyfriend, husband or lover speaks, she will close off her heart to him or only allow him access in certain areas of her heart. Just like the natural heart has many chambers, our supernatural heart (soul) has many levels. To access each level, a man needs to be able to either relate to her, change her mind, or change his mind. If a woman doesn't trust her guy, she will only give him limited access to her heart.

Her Intentions for that Guy

One thing that shocks a lot of men is when I tell them that a woman can marry them, have their children and spend years with them and not have any intentions to spend her life with them. How so? She may be settling for the guy and think that she'd be foolish to let him go.

Additionally, she may have given in to the pressure she's getting from her family and friends to marry the guy, even though she doesn't intend to spend her life with him. In such cases, she will just flow with each day. She'll stick with her guy and make plans with him, all the while, her heart is not fully with him. She's just going along with what's available to her at that moment, but should she be presented with something or someone she prefers more, she will abandon her relationship. The one who got away will be the foundation for every relationship she enters and how she behaves toward each man she romantically links herself to.

One of my friends had given her full heart to a man she'd met while in high school. She loved that man above everything and everyone ... including God. She made an idol out of him, so when they broke up, she was more than broken; she was shattered. She would date other men, but everyone who knew her knew that if "Chaz" had come back, she would hurry up and dump whosoever it was that she was dating. Her obsession with Chaz was pure, unadulterated idolatry. Chaz had been her first lover, but that wasn't necessarily the reason he'd had the greatest effect on her, even though the sex only intensified her obsession with him. He had the greatest effect on her because he'd gone the furthest into her heart. He'd proposed to her and they'd made plans to get married. After Chaz left, their broken relationship was the catalyst that pushed her into the arms of other men. She wasn't as "wild" as my other friends and I at the time, but her failed relationship with Chaz sent her into some really dark places.

Another friend of mine was obsessed with an ex-husband of hers. Even though he hadn't been her first lover, he was obviously the man she felt like she had the greatest connection to. After "Janice" and "Oliver" divorced, Janice went on to have other relationships, but kept finding herself in bed with Oliver. Every man who entered her life felt threatened by Oliver and every woman who entered Oliver's life felt threatened by Janice ... and rightfully so.

Satan isn't just trying to chip away at a woman's heart; he is always looking for that one man who she'll let into the innermost depths of her heart because he wants to use that man to break her heart into minute pieces. That way, he can put her back together the way he wants to put her together. He wants to reshape her mind and open her up for the Jezebel or Delilah spirit ... or both! If she already has either (or both) of these spirits, he wants to increase their influence in her. Additionally, he wants that man to directly or indirectly continue to impact and ruin every relationship that she enters.

Satan gets his power to break a woman when she idolizes a man. Idolatry gives Satan legal access to her mind, will and emotions, but he needs someone to go deeper than he can go. He needs a man who can bypass every sense of reasoning she has and enter the throne room of her heart. This is where God is supposed to be seated. That man will go in and place himself in God's seat and he will operate as a god in her life. Satan will then use him to change the way she thinks, sees, smells, tastes and feel things. He will change her mind so much that she won't be able to recognize herself. Life will be difficult for her when she makes a man her idol, but things will get more complicated once that man makes himself her idol. This means that he will require her to serve him in order to stay with her.

Once Satan has gotten that guy into her heart, he will dethrone him (cause their breakup) and take his place. After all, to Satan, she is potential bait. Her beauty, knowledge, confidence, education level, anointing and connections will all be a determining factor when Satan decides what type of bait he wants her to be and who he wants to use her to catch for himself.

After Satan has performed his biggest break on her, he will send men into her life who will treat her wounded heart, but who are not able to heal it. Every man will go as deep into her heart as she lets him and once Satan decides that he's where he wants him to be, or she won't let him go any further, he will use that guy to break her heart all the more. Satan will then use her brokenness to minister to her. He will tell her that she's too weak, too nice, too trusting or too godly. Basically, he's telling her to be strong against men (become a Jezebel), be meaner, be distrusting and to be more ungodly.

With every break in her heart, her mind will change and so will her physical appearance. She will change her hair and her clothes in an attempt to win back the one who got away, or at least do something to make him regret leaving her. Satan will teach her to wear less clothing and more makeup. This is when he's teaching her to look like and behave like Devil Bait.

Again, this problem didn't start in her relationship with the guy; it started in her heart. She did not make Jesus Christ Lord over her life, even though she may beg to differ. She may have called Him Lord, but she has not yet treated Him as Lord. Instead, she placed someone else on His throne and God allowed that man to show her how lousy of a god a human being will be when that human attempts to take His place.

When a woman makes an idol out of a man, she will then become a living sacrifice. If she has sex with him outside of a legal, godly marriage, she is, in a sense, offering up herself as that sacrifice and whatever she offers her body to him on is the altar. At this point, she has not only given that man access to the throne room of her heart, but she has now escalated in her idolatrous ways. She has given herself as a living sacrifice to him; she has just worshiped the man and this will provoke God all the more because He is a jealous God.

Romans 12:1 (ESV): I appeal to you therefore, brothers, by the mercies of God, to present your bodies as a living sacrifice, holy and acceptable to God, which is your spiritual worship.

2 Corinthians 11:2 (ESV): For I feel a divine jealousy for you, since I betrothed you to one husband, to present you as a pure virgin to Christ.

Anytime a person places an object or person before God, that object or person becomes an idol and idols have to be destroyed. If the relationship is an idol, it won't last. God had a relationship with Israel, but Jezebel turned their hearts away from God and had them worshiping other deities. God then sent Elijah to confront Ahab (Jezebel's husband) and God used Elijah to turn the people's hearts back to Him.

1 Kings 18:17-30 (ESV): When Ahab saw Elijah, Ahab said to him, "Is it you, you troubler of Israel?" And he answered, "I have not troubled Israel, but you have, and your father's house, because you have abandoned the commandments of the Lord and followed the Baals. Now therefore send and gather all Israel to me at Mount Carmel, and the 450 prophets of Baal and the 400 prophets of Asherah, who eat at Jezebel's table."

So Ahab sent to all the people of Israel and gathered the prophets together at Mount Carmel. And Elijah came near to all the people and said, "How long will you go limping between two different opinions? If the Lord is God, follow him; but if Baal, then follow him." And the people did not answer him a word. Then Elijah said to the people, "I, even I only, am left a prophet of the Lord, but Baal's prophets are 450 men. Let

two bulls be given to us, and let them choose
one bull for themselves and cut it in pieces and
lay it on the wood, but put no fire to it. And I will
prepare the other bull and lay it on the wood
and put no fire to it. And you call upon the
name of your god, and I will call upon the name
of the Lord, and the God who answers by fire,
he is God." And all the people answered, "It is
well spoken." Then Elijah said to the prophets of
Baal, "Choose for yourselves one bull and
prepare it first, for you are many, and call upon
the name of your god, but put no fire to it." And
they took the bull that was given them, and
they prepared it and called upon the name of
Baal from morning until noon, saying, "O Baal,
answer us!" But there was no voice, and no
one answered. And they limped around the
altar that they had made. And at noon Elijah
mocked them, saying, "Cry aloud, for he is a
god. Either he is musing, or he is relieving
himself, or he is on a journey, or perhaps he is
asleep and must be awakened." And they cried
aloud and cut themselves after their custom

with swords and lances, until the blood gushed out upon them. And as midday passed, they raved on until the time of the offering of the oblation, but there was no voice. No one answered; no one paid attention.

Then Elijah said to all the people, "Come near to me." And all the people came near to him. And he repaired the altar of the Lord that had been thrown down.

The point is that many women aren't victims of the men who've hurt them; they are simply women who've limped and shouted around the wrong altars until they came to realize that their god couldn't do anything on his own. They were forced to acknowledge the one and true living God: YAHWEH. The ones who didn't repent became angrier and Satan simply built another altar for them to limp around. It won't be long before they realize that they are the sacrifices on those altars and Satan has no plans to give them the desires of their wicked hearts. He just wants to use them as bait.

Jeremiah 17:9 (KJV): The heart is deceitful above all things, and desperately wicked: who can know it?

A Woman's Attire

A woman's attire has always communicated
with those who came in contact with her.
There were garments worn by virgins, married
women, widows and prostitutes. It was a
dishonor, for example, for a non-virgin (married
woman) to wear the garments of a virgin.
Such an act could be considered misleading and
seen as her attempt to deceive others.

Outward appearances by both men and
women were used as a means of non-verbal
communications. A good example would be a
man who'd just received bad news. He would
rent, or better yet, tear his clothes to display
his grief or anger. Another example would be
sackcloth. Sackcloth was often worn by men
who were fasting or grieving. Men who usually
rent their clothes would put on sackcloth.
Additionally, just like today, there were

garments considered to be the garments of wealthy men, just like there were garments considered to be those worn by poor men. When Jacob gave his son, Joseph, a coat of many colors, he gave him a garment that was similar to the coats that royal men wore at that time.

As we see, clothing, in that era, was symbolic of one's beliefs, emotional state, relationship status, and wealth. Of course, the same is true of many of today's believers and non-believers.

Prostitutes were known to not only cover their faces, but they wore costly apparel and jewelry. They were known to adorn themselves with pearls and gold, and this was to make themselves more appealing to their potential customers. For this reason, Apostle Paul wrote, "I desire then that in every place the men should pray, lifting holy hands without anger or quarreling; likewise also that women should adorn themselves in respectable apparel, with modesty and self-control, not with braided hair and gold or pearls or costly attire, but with what is proper for women who profess godliness—with good works" (1 Timothy 2:8-15 ESV).

Prostitutes were known to adorn themselves in expensive, intricate clothing so they could draw attention to themselves and get more customers. Apostle Paul made it clear that the women of God, and not just those in the church in Ephesus, should place more emphasis on holiness than external beauty.

Again, clothing was (and still is) used to communicate a message to onlookers. A prostitute in biblical times did not wear fancy clothing to compete with moral women; she wore it to compete with other prostitutes. She understood that a man looking to have a one-night-stand was going to choose the woman who was most appealing to three of his senses: sight, smell, and hearing. For this reason, prostitutes often wore fancy hairstyles, jewelry and perfume. They also chose their words carefully. Women then and now understood the power of words and the seductive sounds and pitches that were most appealing to men. Paul warned the women in Ephesus (and Christian women altogether) to refrain from taking on the mindsets and ways of prostitutes. Because Christ had done away with the Old Testament Law, it was necessary to remind the people of what was good in the eyes of God.

Nowadays, it is the norm to see a scantily clad woman walking about in general society. The reason for this is that today's media now glamorizes sexual immorality. Moral women are often depicted as snooty, religious, uptight, judgmental, boring men-haters who loathe sex and love to gossip. Immoral women are depicted as down-to-earth, reasonable, fun-loving, open-minded and non-judgmental. They are also portrayed as beautiful, seductive

creatures who love sex and understand men.
Of course, this is a misrepresentation of both
moral and immoral women. It goes without
saying that there are some religious, uptight,
men-hating Jezebels who loathe sex and
profess themselves to be Christians, but these
women do not represent true Christian women.
This reminds me of what I heard from a few
African men and women during the time that I
was married to an African man. I was under
the impression that the majority of the people
on the African continent lived in poverty. This is
because I'd lived a sheltered life and had never
traveled abroad, nor had I ever personally met
someone from Africa before I'd met and
married my ex. I remember a few people
(including my ex) telling me that America and
other western countries had intentionally
portrayed Africa as a poor nation in dire need
of their help. This portrayal could help greedy
Americans and Westerners to disguise their
presence in many African countries as
missionary work, when in truth, they were

stealing the wealth from Africa. This misrepresentation of the African continent allowed many bloodthirsty and greedy Westerners to silently invade Africa, steal its wealth, rape its women and get away with its crimes by disguising themselves as people who'd come to help the nation. The same rings true for Jezebels disguising themselves as Christian women. We must understand that these women are demon-possessed or demonically influenced to enter the church and rob it of its wealth and good reputation. We must always test the spirits in the people we meet because there are two types of people out: those who represent the god (or gods) they worship and those who misrepresent God. A true Christian is a representative of YAHWEH, but a hypocrite represents his or her god by misrepresenting the true and living God, YAHWEH. Our clothes are the first indicators of who we represent.

One of the most interesting stories in the Bible

involved another woman by the name of Tamar, and ironically enough, this story also involves sexual immorality.

Tamar was the daughter of King David. King David had many wives, but only eight of them were mentioned in the Bible. Tamar's mother was named Maach. Maach also had a son with David and his name was Absalom.

One of David's wives (Ahinoham) bore him a son named Amnon and Amnon was a wicked man. 2 Samuel 13:1-19 tells the horrific story of Tamar's life-changing encounter with her half-brother, Amnon.

2 Samuel 13:1-19 (ESV): Now Absalom, David's son, had a beautiful sister, whose name was Tamar. And after a time Amnon, David's son, loved her. And Amnon was so tormented that he made himself ill because of his sister Tamar, for she was a virgin, and it seemed impossible to Amnon to do anything to her. But Amnon had a friend, whose name was Jonadab, the son of Shimeah, David's brother. And Jonadab was a very crafty man. And he said to him, "O son of the king, why are you so haggard morning after morning? Will you not tell me?" Amnon said to him, "I love Tamar, my brother Absalom's sister." Jonadab said to him, "Lie down on your bed and pretend to be ill. And when your father comes to see you, say to him, 'Let my sister Tamar come and give me bread to eat, and prepare the food in my sight, that I may see it and eat it from her hand.'" So Amnon lay down and pretended to be ill. And when the king came to see him, Amnon said to the king, "Please let my sister Tamar come and make a couple of cakes in my sight, that I may eat from her hand."

Then David sent home to Tamar, saying, "Go to your brother Amnon's house and prepare food for him." So Tamar went to her brother Amnon's house, where he was lying down. And she took dough and kneaded it and made cakes in his sight and baked the cakes. And she took the pan and emptied it out before him, but he refused to eat. And Amnon said, "Send out everyone from me." So everyone went out from him. Then Amnon said to Tamar, "Bring the food into the chamber, that I may eat from your hand." And Tamar took the cakes she had made and brought them into the chamber to Amnon her brother. But when she brought them near him to eat, he took hold of her and said to her, "Come, lie with me, my sister." She answered him, "No, my brother, do not violate me, for such a thing is not done in Israel; do not do this outrageous thing. As for me, where could I carry my shame? And as for you, you would be as one of the outrageous fools in Israel. Now therefore, please speak to the king, for he will not withhold me from you." But he would not listen to her, and being stronger than she, he violated her and lay with her.

Then Amnon hated her with very great hatred, so that the hatred with which he hated her was greater than the love with which he had loved her. And Amnon said to her, "Get up! Go!" But she said to him, "No, my brother, for this wrong in sending me away is greater than the other that you did to me." But he would not listen to her. He called the young man who served him and said, "Put this woman out of my presence and bolt the door after her." Now she was wearing a long robe with sleeves, for thus were the virgin daughters of the king dressed. So his servant put her out and bolted the door after her. And Tamar put ashes on her head and tore the long robe that she wore. And she laid her hand on her head and went away, crying aloud as she went.

There is a lot that we can take from this story, but I want to draw your attention to the following:

1. Amnon did not ask David for Tamar's hand in marriage.
2. Tamar begged Amnon to ask David for her hand in marriage, rather than rape her.
3. Before raping Tamar, Amnon is said to have "loved" his sister and this "love" was tormenting to him. After the rape,

Amnon hated his sister.

4. After raping her, Amnon tried to send Tamar away, but she didn't want to go. She said that sending her away was worse than the rape itself.

5. When Tamar was kicked out of Amnon's room, she tore her robe and put ashes on her head.

Every one of these points is important because they explain the Jewish cultures and beliefs of that time.

1. **Amnon did not ask David for Tamar's hand in marriage**: If Amnon was sure that he loved Tamar, he would have asked for her hand in marriage. Instead, Amnon's love was sensual or, better yet, he lusted after Tamar. For this reason, he did not want to marry Tamar; he wanted to have sex with her. When Tamar refused his advances, he raped her because his lust for her had grown into obsession. A man can be obsessed

with a woman to the point where he thinks that he loves her, but the truth is, his desire for her is sensual in nature. This is how so many children are born out of wedlock and why so many divorces take place today. When ministering to brokenhearted women, I often tell them that the men who broke their hearts were probably being truthful when they said that they "loved" them. The problem is ... they didn't know what type of love they had, and being that they were not saved and had no knowledge of true "Agape" love, they confused Eros (romantic love) with Agape (unconditional love). Once their flesh had been repeatedly appeased, they could not back up their claim to love them because a man will not want to be financially or morally responsible for a woman that he does not love with Agape love (unconditionally). This is unless, of course, he can have her as a sensual lover (concubine), all the while, having a wife to bear his last name.

2. **Tamar begged Amnon to ask David for her hand in marriage, rather than rape her:** Even though incest was against the Old Testament Law, it was far better than being labeled a harlot. Tamar understood that Amnon's act could bring shame to their father's name; plus, she would be considered a woman who'd "played the whore in her father's house." This act alone could have gotten her stoned.

3. **Before raping Tamar, Amnon is said to have "loved" his sister and this "love" was tormenting to him. After the rape, Amnon hated his sister:** Of course, what Amnon had for Tamar was not true, godly love or the love from a husband to a wife. It was lust; it was the very desire that drives a man to lie with a prostitute. For this reason, Amnon had a change of heart once he'd

gotten what he wanted from Tamar and he refused to cover her as a husband after he'd uncovered her like a wife. This is common with today's youth. Many men and women believe that they love the people they are romantically linked to, but once their lusts have been fulfilled, they find themselves entertaining a different set of emotions.

4. **After raping her, Amnon tried to send Tamar away, but she didn't want to go. She said that sending her away was worse than the rape itself:** This may first come across as baffling; after all, why would a woman want to stay near her rapist and why would she say that sending her away was worse than the rape itself? To understand this, we must understand the Old Testament Law and Jewish customs. By refusing to marry her (legally), Amnon was treating her as a whore. At the same time, he didn't care that his behavior could bring

shame to his father. Additionally, Tamar could no longer wear the garments of a virgin, thus publicly acknowledging that she was not a virgin. Of course, everyone would notice that she wasn't wearing the garments of a married woman, which meant her sex was illegal. In other words, she would regard herself as a whore and this could have gotten her killed if she had not screamed and identified her rapist. This put Tamar in a sensitive position: acknowledge that she'd been raped, which would mean that her hateful brother would be forced to marry her and her dad's name would be blemished or live a life of shame. She chose the latter.

5. **When Tamar was kicked out of Amnon's room, she tore her robe and put ashes on her head:** Tamar tore her robe for two reasons. One reason was she had come into the room wearing a virgin's garment, but upon leaving, she

was no longer a virgin. Secondly, Tamar tore her robe, put ashes on her head and began to cry loudly as an expression of her grief. She was publicly acknowledging that she'd been raped, even though this acknowledgment was in a controlled environment: her father's home.

Another remarkable thing occurred in this story. Absalom, Tamar's full brother, saw her walking away with her robe torn, ashes on her head and crying loudly. He knew then that she'd been raped. But instead of addressing her rapist, Absalom told Tamar to keep her peace, or better yet, to be quiet about the matter. He then took her in his house. Of course, there was a reason for this.

2 Samuel 13:20-22 (ESV): And her brother Absalom said to her, "Has Amnon your brother been with you? Now hold your peace, my sister. He is your brother; do not take this to heart." So Tamar lived, a desolate woman, in her brother Absalom's house. When King David heard of all these things, he was very angry. But Absalom spoke to Amnon neither good nor bad, for Absalom hated Amnon, because he had violated his sister Tamar.

Why did Absalom tell Tamar to hold her peace? He expected justice from his father. The news got back to David about the rape and the Bible recounts that David was angry, however, he did not punish his son for the deed. This was an error on David's part and it could have meant that Absalom would be morally and financially responsible for his sister for the rest of his life. I'm sure he didn't mind taking care of his sister, but at the same time, he wanted Amnon to pay for what he did. When David didn't punish Amnon for his treacherous act, Absalom decided to take matters into his own hands.

2 Samuel 13:23-29 (ESV): After two full years Absalom had sheepshearers at Baal-hazor, which is near Ephraim, and Absalom invited all the king's sons. And Absalom came to the king and said, "Behold, your servant has sheepshearers. Please let the king and his servants go with your servant." But the king said to Absalom, "No, my son, let us not all go, lest we be burdensome to you." He pressed him, but he would not go but gave him his blessing. Then Absalom said, "If not, please let my brother Amnon go with us." And the king said to him, "Why should he go with you?" But Absalom pressed him until he let Amnon and all the king's sons go with him. Then Absalom commanded his servants, "Mark when Amnon's heart is merry with wine, and when I say to you, 'Strike Amnon,' then kill him. Do not fear; have I not commanded you? Be courageous and be valiant." So the servants of Absalom did to Amnon as Absalom had commanded. Then all the king's sons arose, and each mounted his mule and fled.

Why did Absalom wait two years to kill Amnon? He likely waited for his father to punish Amnon or he was hoping that Amnon would acknowledge his wrongs and honor Tamar by marrying her. Instead, Amnon went on with his life and David pretended that the act had never happened. Absalom felt it was his duty to carry out justice and restore honor to his sister's name.

By murdering Amnon, Absalom restored honor to his sister and he freed her so that she could someday get (legally) married and have children. As long as Amnon was alive, Tamar could not marry another man. This meant that if Amnon had lived to be an old man, Tamar would have lived shamefully in her brother's house, never to have children. Needless to say, Amnon could go on and marry as many women as he wanted.

After two years, Absalom could safely acknowledge that Amnon had no intentions of doing the honorary thing; plus, David had no intentions of making Amnon pay for his crime against Tamar. For this reason, Absalom killed Amnon and went into exile. As the story continues, David longed for his son, Absalom, and wanted him to return, however, Absalom began to despise his father. He conspired to have him killed and this led to Absalom's death.

I suspect that David forgave Absalom so easily because he understood why Absalom killed Amnon. At the same time, he knew that he'd let Absalom and Tamar down by not punishing Amnon for his crime. The proper thing to have done, according to Jewish customs, was to force Amnon to marry Tamar, but David didn't do that.

Deuteronomy 22:28-29 (ESV): If a man meets a virgin who is not betrothed, and seizes her and lies with her, and they are found, then the man who lay with her shall give to the father of the young woman fifty shekels of silver, and she shall be his wife, because he has violated her. He may not divorce her all his days.

Tamar was a good example of a moral woman who sought to do the right thing, but she fell into the hands of an evil man. Additionally, David's refusal to punish Amnon opened the door for a division to be birthed in his family that would eventually lead to the deaths of both of his sons: Amnon and Absalom. Amnon died because he'd raped his sister. Absalom died because he'd began to despise the father who neglected to punish the man who'd raped his sister. Remember that Absalom and Tamar had the same mother. This meant that their bond was stronger than that of the bond between Absalom and Amnon. Of course, Absalom tried to take his father's kingdom from him and one of his acts was to publicly defile some of David's wives on the roof of his palace. The Bible says he did this in the sight of all Israel; meaning he carried on a public pornographic show.

It would be interesting to know what Tamar wore for the two years that Amnon was alive.

As with Jewish customs, once Amnon was dead, she likely wore the garments of a widow. She likely closed herself up in Absalom's house while Amnon was alive and she didn't have any resolve in the matter because David didn't address what had happened to her. It is possible that she wore the clothing of a woman in grieving at that time, but the Bible gives us no more information about Tamar after her rape.

Today, women still use their clothing to communicate with onlookers. For example, some religions wear clothing that helps general society to identify the religion that they are submitted to. Promiscuous and immoral women oftentimes wear fitted garments to bring attention to their bodies. They also wear clothes that reveal their breasts, thighs, and buttocks. They do this to send a message to men and that message isn't always that they want to have sex. Nowadays, many sexually immoral women wear skimpy clothes hoping to attract husbands to themselves. Because of pride, they would argue that their clothes are simply an expression of their confidence in their bodies, but the truth of the matter is most women who wear revealing and fitted clothing do so to get attention. They do this to draw husbands to themselves and to rebuild their self-esteem. After all, society has torn down women for years and these days, many women look in the mirror and measure themselves according to society's rule of beauty. When they feel they don't measure up, they compete with what Hollywood (and general media) depicts as a beautiful and desired woman. Unfortunately, in this day and age, Hollywood portrays immoral, ungodly women as the new standard of beauty. Great examples of this deception is the over-glamorization of women such as Marilyn Monroe and Kim Kardashian.

Marilyn Monroe was a beautiful, yet seductive actress and model who became one of the most popular sex symbols of her time. She was mostly known for her alleged affair with then-president, John F. Kennedy and her seductive performance at his birthday party. Hollywood had long begun to capitalize off the glamorization of immoral women by then and Marilyn Monroe was just another woman they exploited for capital gain.

Kim Kardashian's father, Robert Kardashian, represented O.J. Simpson at his murder trial; plus, she was close friends with Paris Hilton, another rich and immoral woman who'd used sex to propel herself to super stardom. Nevertheless, Kim wasn't famous because of her father or her best friend; her rise to fame came after she'd recorded a pornographic video with an actor and performer who went by the stage name of Ray J. Leaked sex tapes had become a trend and every star who was propelled to super stardom through the release of a pornographic video claimed to be distraught about the release of their videos. Nevertheless, it is common knowledge that

most of these releases were not accidental;
they were the attempts of sinking and not-so-
famous actors and actresses to capture or
recapture the attention of Hollywood and their
disinterested fans. As we can see, most of
these attempts were very successful. Why did
they do this? A common adage today is: sex
sells. We live in a perverted society that has
an immoral obsession with beauty and sex.
When you put the two together, you have a
society that is obsessed with beautiful, immoral
women who are willing to do anything to gain
popularity and grow their bank accounts. What
we have is what can best be described as
peep-show prostitution. Those who lust after
such women pay to see more of them.
Consider the shrine prostitutes of the biblical
days. They would live in shrines that were built
to honor demons (Baal, Tammuz and Asherah).
They would have sex with the men at the
shrines in honor of their gods, but of course,
those men had to pay for this pleasure.
Oftentimes, this was done when the men

entered the temple and paid for their sacrificial offering of a bull, goat, lamb or chicken. The men didn't necessarily pay for the women, even though the women came with the worship experience. They paid to worship their deities and the women were just bonuses.

Nowadays, the same rings true with Hollywood. People pay to watch movies and be entertained, but immoral women are oftentimes cast in the films as a bonus and to draw more viewers. Women like Marilyn Monroe and Kim Kardashian are nothing but sex symbols used by Hollywood to fatten their own pockets. Of course, if you offer to pay an immoral woman to do immoral things, she will not turn you down.

Marilyn Monroe was often portrayed as a "dumb blonde" in the movies she acted in and Kim Kardashian is almost always depicted as a beautiful, seductive woman who knows her way around a mall. Hollywood has made a very clear statement about its views of women, but many refuse to see this. Nevertheless, our culture demands more women with less clothing and the media is all-too-eager to give them what they want. Again, clothing communicates a message and unfortunately, the message our generation is communicating is that it is immoral, perverted, ungodly, sex-obsessed and demeaning towards women. The worst part is ... many of our women today are playing along with this message.

Morally Unsound

When I was in the world, I was, without question, an immoral woman. This could be seen in the clothes I wore, heard in the words I chose and witnessed in my many relationships. Not only was I immoral, but my friends were immoral. Even though we chose different paths in immorality, we were the infamous "birds of a feather who flocked together." Truthfully, I can look back now and say that we were all fascinated with each other's immoral ways. This is why we would gather together to discuss our trysts. It was during that time that I learned about the different types of immoral women. I had friends who unashamedly referred to themselves as "whores." Then again, I had friends who were even more promiscuous than the ones who openly confessed what they were and they would get offended at any implication that they were immoral. They coped with their heart's conditions by denying them. Finally, there were the ones who simply didn't say if they believed that they were or were not promiscuous. I was a woman who'd loudly proclaim my innocence. I didn't want to believe that I was a whore. After all, my generation had redefined the word "whore" and the new, hip word was "ho." I believed that a "ho" was a woman who had multiple sex partners at one time or within a short period of time. This was the common belief for many of the women who grew up in the eighties and nineties.

Somehow, Satan managed to convince me that if I stretched my whoredom out and if I had sex under the "girlfriend" title that I wasn't a whore. So, I went from one relationship to the next, often taking a few months off between relationships to maintain the reputation that I wanted to have. I tried hard to not think about what I was or what I was becoming because that meant that my already wounded self-perception would have to take another hit. Nevertheless, I could not ignore the fact that my relationships were lasting six months or less and the number of men I'd had sex with was growing. I would often write down the names of the men I'd been romantically linked to, and at first, this wasn't a problem because I hadn't had sex with the majority of the men on that list. I was lost, broken and prideful, so my list was the equivalent of a man's black book. I would think about how handsome each man was and I'd revel in the fact that I'd once been his girlfriend; plus, I'd been the one who'd rejected him. This was the evidence that I myself was a rejected soul who dealt with rejection by rejecting men before they could reject me. As time went on, I could no longer write down the names because I started noticing that my sexual encounters had grown so I could no longer take pride in my list. After all, sex followed by a break-up spelled out a message to me that I did not want to hear.

I dressed provocatively everywhere I went because I liked the attention I got from men. Now that I am honest with myself, I can say that the attention that I craved was simply my way of responding to every failed relationship that I had been a part of. I would often brag about the fact that I'd been the one who'd ended each relationship, but this was just a mask I wore to disguise my shame. The truth is that I ended those relationships because I felt rejected by my lovers or I sensed rejection heading my way. If they cheated, I rejected them. If their attitudes towards me became cold or they became distant, I rejected them. If they flirted with other women, I rejected them. If their ex-girlfriends were a part of their lives, I rejected them. I had friends who would repeatedly find themselves in serious relationships and I watched them be humiliated and hurt time and time again, so I decided that I didn't want to be like them. I did this because secretly, I knew that I could not handle the rejection. In my pride, I thought I was stronger

than they were, but truthfully, I was a coward.
I was scared of the idea of loving someone only
to have him reject me.

What most of my friends didn't know was that
I'd let my guard down when I was a teenager
and I'd gotten my heart broken. What's worse
is that our relationship didn't last long enough
for me to justify my obsession with my former
lover. We'd only dated a few months, but
when we broke up, I didn't know how to handle
the emotions so I obsessed over him for two
years. I was so lost and broken that I even
called psychic hotlines to see if there was any
chance that we'd reconcile. Even when I
entered new relationships, I would often say in
my heart that if my ex called that I would end
the relationship I was in to get back with him.
I'd experienced what it was like to be humbled
and I didn't like it, so I spent the next few years
running from love. Truthfully, I wanted love and
marriage, but I didn't know how to go about
getting it; plus, I was terrified of romantic

rejection. Prideful people are, in most cases, slaves of people bondage and I was no different. I didn't want to deal with the humiliation of being rejected, especially after exalting myself to others. It was all a lie; it was a facade. I knew a lot about men and what I knew told me that I was the very thing that I was fighting not to become.

One of the most notable attempts I made to avoid the "whore" label involved my relationship with a man who we'll call Wyatt. Wyatt wasn't the type of man who I would ordinarily attract at that stage in my life. As a matter of fact, I credit him with being the one who made me leave thugs alone altogether. After him, the type of men I dated were more of what we called "suit and tie" kind of guys.

Wyatt was handsome, successful and sexually immoral. I was 18 or 19 when I came in contact with Wyatt and I didn't believe that I was his type. After all, my family was poor and I didn't

fit the type of woman I believed Wyatt went for.
I reasoned within myself that Wyatt's type
would be a fair-skinned woman with long hair
who came from a successful family. Believe it
or not, many women reason like this and this
helps them to determine how to define their
roles with the men they romantically link
themselves to.

Even though I didn't believe that I was Wyatt's
type, I was extremely attracted to him. To me,
he was like a celebrity, not because he was
handsome (I had a list of handsome men I'd
dated), but because he was different. Wyatt
was debonair, or what we called "classy." He
looked like he'd been torn from the pages of a
magazine and I didn't want to pass up the
opportunity to have some type of experience
with him. But again, I didn't think I was his type,
even though he was expressing interest in me.
Honestly, I was beyond scared of letting Wyatt
anywhere near my heart. I could honestly say
what was in me recognized what was in him.

Because of this, I told myself the truth about Wyatt. I told myself that he was "out there"; meaning he was a man-whore. I told myself that he wouldn't know how to be faithful to a woman if she was the only woman on Earth and I told myself that Wyatt wanted sex from me. How could I keep Wyatt away from my heart, but still link myself to him romantically? After all, I could tell that Wyatt was a hopeless romantic. The idea came to me while I was sitting in the passenger's seat of his car. I'd been trying to avoid the "whore-tag" and a new hit song had me convinced that I needed to have a boy toy of my own. I reasoned with myself that men did this, so why would it be wrong for me to do it? Without warning, I told Wyatt what I wanted from him. I explained to him that I had been going from one relationship to the next and I didn't want to be labeled a "ho". I told him that I knew he wasn't the faithful type, so I wanted to have a no-strings-attached sexual relationship with him between any formal or informal relationship I found myself in. I was addicted to sex and I knew it. With this arrangement, I believed that I could have normal, sexless relationships with other men and when those relationships ended, I could satisfy my lusts and my need to feel wanted by calling Wyatt. I could also repair the damage done to my ego (by other failed relationships) by calling Wyatt. If the relationship wasn't serious, I could call Wyatt to prevent myself from becoming sexually involved with whatever man I was seeing. I knew that if I'd gotten sexually involved with whatever boyfriend I had, I would not have sex with Wyatt; after all, according to my warped thinking, sleeping with two men in the same time frame would automatically qualify me as a whore.

Wyatt and I "honored" this agreement for a few years. He didn't ask too many questions about my love life and I didn't ask questions about his. I would often go months without calling Wyatt and vice versa. When we did speak, our

conversations were short and to the point.
"Are you available?" or "Can I come over?" My
friends envied my boldness because I was in a
conservative state (Mississippi) that was
guarded by many traditional values, but I was
acting like a whore out of Hollywood. This
relationship changed me and I started dating
men who were "suit and tie" types. I became
bolder, more arrogant and before long, I
stopped thinking that I wasn't a man's type of
girl.

Amazingly enough, as unsound as my
reasoning was, it is the reasoning of many
immoral women. Women often measure
themselves by:
- what their families say about them.
- what their peers say about them.
- the general standard of beauty as
  defined by their generation and/ or
  environment.
- their economic status.
- the women represented in the media

culture they have involved themselves in or were born into.

- their sexual history.
- and what they believe about themselves.
- what their lovers or former lovers have said about them.

With each failed relationship, my pride grew because my self-esteem had taken another hit. I became more and more intolerant, impatient and controlling. I didn't realize it then, but I was a Delilah being groomed by the Jezebel spirit. The ingredients for the Jezebel were all present: rejection, hurt, unforgiveness, distrust, sexual immorality and control. All of these things were secured by pride and the belief that I was justified in being the way I was.

Jezebel versus Delilah

I was eight years old and I was obsessed with the artist, Prince. If I heard his voice, I'd run to find the television or radio ... whichever media player his voice was coming out of. I was bewitched by him to the point where I fantasized about being his wife. I believed with my whole heart that I would someday be his wife. It's sad to say that this was the heart of an eight-year-old little girl.

When Prince came out with the movie, Purple Rain, I insisted that my parents buy the movie for me on video tape. I don't remember if they bought it or if someone recorded it for us, but what I do remember is I had that tape and I played it very often. Of course, after watching the movie, I became obsessed with his then girlfriend, Apollonia.

My obsession with Apollonia was not of a romantic nature (of course). I was obsessed with her beauty and the fact that Prince wanted her. I studied her and I wanted to be like her, so I learned to dance seductively like her. If my dad hadn't been around, I would have even dressed like her. When he wasn't at home, I would find the shortest skirt in my possession and wear it. *I'd gotten most of my clothes as hand-me-downs from some of my cousins.*

There was a 24-year-old man who lived across the street from me. He was the uncle of my best friend; we will call him "Cliff." Cliff behaved like Prince, dressed like a combination of Michael Jackson and Prince and was really good at playing the guitar. Cliff was a talented pedophile.

Cliff would often flirt with me whenever I went to visit my friend, "Jocelyn". He would sing and dance for me and he would often refer to me as his "girlfriend". He reminded me of Prince and because of this, I had a huge crush on him. Nevertheless, an eight-year-old crush is not the same as the crush an adult woman has. I wanted him to sing and dance for me, and I wanted him to marry me when I got old enough. I'd seen a lot of kissing on television, so I was sure I wanted him to kiss me, but I was far too afraid of that. So, I just wanted him to stick to playing that guitar and singing.

Thankfully, Cliff never got the chance to molest me. The furthest he'd gone was to kiss me, but my dad sensed Cliff's intentions and forbade me from going across the street to his house. This didn't stop me from trying to woo Cliff with the seductive dances I'd learned watching Apollonia and other artists. So, one day, I went outside and stood on the driveway. (Our house was directly across the street from Cliff's parents' house, which was where he was living). I was hoping that Cliff was looking out his window at me. I began to dance seductively because I didn't understand that my moves were affiliated with sex. I just thought I was a good dancer and men liked women who danced the way I danced. Unfortunately for me, my dad came home early and caught me. That's when I got the spanking of my life.

As I got older, I continued to watch MTV and BET to learn how I should act, dress and dance. Little did I know, Satan was teaching me to become a temptress.

I thought I was learning to become a man's dream woman. I thought that I'd have a lot of men fawning over me and I'd get to choose the one I wanted to spend my life with. Little did I know, Satan would have a lot of men fawning over me, but not the whole me ... only parts of me. At the same time, Satan never trains a seductress to be a wife; it is not his intention that she be a monogamous woman married to a monogamous man. To him, she is nothing but Devil Bait.

The more ungodly I became, the more men praised my ways. It wasn't long before I discovered that my proud, feisty and controlling ways made me more attractive to men. The meaner I was, the more gifts and compliments I received. What the enemy was doing was disciplining me to walk in the role he'd assigned me to and that was the role of a strong Delilah. People often think that the Jezebel spirit is the strongest spirit and because of this, they often mislabel a woman carrying a Delilah spirit as one who is bound by a Jezebel spirit. For this reason, many women in the church are often delivered from the Jezebel spirit, but they are not delivered from the Delilah spirit. This is why you see so many women in church (including leaders) dressing seductively and going from one relationship to the next. The truth is that the enemy will often place both the Delilah and the Jezebel spirits in a woman, but the Delilah will be the strongman if the woman can seduce men with her outer appearance. Jezebel will be the strongman if the woman can attract men of notable authority because Jezebel seeks to rob a man of his authority and rule over whomsoever that man was given charge over.

The reason Satan likes to use the Delilah as the strongman or the ruling demon is because it is easier for him to consume a man if he knows the source of that man's strength. Delilah will weaken a man just enough for Satan to consume him.

Proverbs 6:26 (KJV): For by means of a whorish woman a man is brought to a piece of bread: and the adulteress will hunt for the precious life.

1 Peter 5:8 (ESV): Be sober-minded; be watchful. Your adversary the devil prowls around like a roaring lion, seeking someone to devour.

Jezebel is often nicknamed the "bride of Satan" because that spirit has a reputation for being vicious, manipulative, controlling and merciless. Howbeit, when I had that spirit, anyone who came in contact with me would need to be very discerning to detect it because I appeared to be passive, soft-spoken and kind. Jezebel wasn't my strongman; that demon was there to help Delilah swallow up the men who came my way. Sure, I could be feisty and dominating, but for the most part, I was really sweet. I had a chameleon spirit; I could easily determine what I needed to be according to the man I was romantically involved with. With one man, I could be sweet, loving, and understanding. With another man, I could be mean, neglectful and intolerant. This is how demons behave. They will detect what types of spirits a man is bound by and then, send out a spirit or several spirits that relate to the ones he's in submission to. For example, if a man bound by an Ahab spirit had come in contact with me, the Jezebel spirit would have come out to engage with him. If a man who walked in confidence and authority came after me, the Delilah spirit would have engaged with him. Because Jezebel wasn't my strongman, I oftentimes avoided

Ahabs. I didn't like what I believed to be weak men. I liked men of authority, men like Samson in the Bible.

If I had gone to a church and undergone deliverance, the one performing the deliverance would have needed to be very knowledgeable about the Delilah spirit. They would truly need to hear from God to know what I had, otherwise, they would have cast Jezebel out and left Delilah.

The Delilah spirit gives a woman supernatural knowledge about a man. Most of my friends were Delilahs and we all knew which men we could have and which ones we could not have. I could often be heard saying that I could have any man I wanted, regardless of his marital status or religious convictions. Did I believe this? Yes, for the most part, I did. Nevertheless, if I came in contact with a man who walked in holiness, I knew I couldn't have him. To me, he was one of a kind. The same was true for my friends. They knew they could entice a large number of men, but they also knew who was "guarded." How did we know the difference between a supernaturally guarded man versus a man who was not so guarded? Men who aren't fully delivered have wandering eyes and they don't have to stare at a woman lustfully for her to see this. All she needs to do is look into their eyes and she will identify something familiar in them. Sometimes, a man can be a decent man who wants to love and protect his family, but because he has unchecked sin in his heart, he will find himself on Delilah's menu.

I preferred single men, but many of my friends preferred married men. Some of us worked in retail and one sign of unchecked sin was if a man felt the need to take a second look at one of us. It didn't matter if he wore a mean expression on his face or if he was mean to us. We could look in his eyes and see that he was not guarded. Of course, we didn't know that what we had was demonic knowledge; we simply knew how to differentiate a faithful man from a not-so-faithful one. Delilah senses a man's weakness, but she won't necessarily know the fullness of it until she understands his strength.

Most women who have Delilah spirits are very seductive and manipulative. Delilahs play on a man's weakness by appearing to be weak herself. Jezebel tests a man's strength by appearing to be strong. A woman with a Delilah spirit will oftentimes be a great listener. She appeals to a man's need to protect the weak, so she pretends to be helpless and weak herself. By doing this, she discovers and uncovers the source of his strength.

A great example of a Delilah spirit could be seen through a church's sexually immoral secretary who patiently listens to her pastor talk about the problems he's having in his marriage. Most people would write such a woman off as a Jezebel, but in truth, in most cases, she is a Delilah. She will encourage her leader to buy roses for his wife, take his wife on spontaneous dates and surprise his wife with gifts. *This is manipulation at its best.* What she's doing is getting him to trust her by pretending to help him fix the problems in his marriage. Additionally, unbeknownst to him, she is getting him to reveal the source of his strength. She will come off as a great friend, listener, intercessor and the perfect woman. She will also pretend to be supportive of his wife. This can be confusing to a man who notices his wife's disdain for the secretary, especially since he believes the secretary is fond of his wife. In truth, most women (both saved and unsaved) can detect this spirit, but most men cannot.

Jezebels can be just as manipulative as Delilahs, but they won't always use seduction to get what they want. Jezebels use fear, intimidation and coercion. I had a friend whose strongman was the Jezebel spirit and she was more controlling than she was seductive. She preferred to use her emotions to get what she wanted, and this was largely due to the fact that she wasn't as confident as my other friends.

Many women today embrace the Delilah spirit because they believe that seduction will help them to get and keep the men of their dreams. This is pure deception. Delilah is not a spirit assigned to "keep" a man; her assignment is to expose the source of his strength to his enemy. Delilah is designed to get the man, expose the man, and then lose the man ... contrary to popular belief. Jezebel, on the other hand, has a more lengthy assignment. Her goal is to remove the headship (authority) from the man, emasculate that man repeatedly and bear children for him who are essentially without a covering.

1 Corinthians 11:3 (ESV): But I want you to understand that the head of every man is Christ, the head of a wife is her husband, and the head of Christ is God.

By removing the man's authority, Jezebel removes the headship of Christ. This allows her to take authority over all of his possessions and the people he has authority over (his children, church congregation, employees, etc.). This also allows her to give birth to Athaliah, Ahaziah and Jehoram. These spirits cannot be born until the Baal order is established in a household. In God's order, Christ is the head of man and the man is the head of his wife, or better yet, his household. The Baal system perverts this order, thus making the woman equal to or greater than her husband. Now, this isn't to say that women are inferior to men in God's eyes because they aren't. This is to say that the headship or managerial spot in a home was assigned to the husband by God. This position is a position of great responsibility and every man who dishonors his wife and abuses his authority is judged by the Lord since Jesus is his head. The marital order was also demonstrated in the Old Testament, whereas fathers gave their daughters away in marriage and the new husband took the position of protecting and providing for his wife. He could determine where they lived, what god they served and where they lived. Of course, Satan perverted this order by causing some men to abuse their authority, desert their families and abuse their wives. These behaviors were further exposed by the media and this caused the birth of many feminist movements. Women began to demand to be equal to men in the workplace and in society in general. The truth is that some men did not know how to be the heads of their homes, so they abandoned, mistreated and abused their wives. Many women were forced to live beneath the poverty level when their husbands deserted them to be with other women. To make matters worse, it was hard for women to get jobs outside of teaching jobs because women were seen as motherly and weak. Women began to demand equal opportunities, equal pay and to be seen as equal all across the board. Now, there is nothing wrong with women wanting equal pay, equal opportunities and so on, but the problem came in when many women began to take authority over their husbands. This was largely due to the pain and distrust brought on by the growing epidemic of family desertion by husbands. Understand this: when a man leaves his home to be with another woman, it is because he is under the influence of the Ahab spirit and he's under the spell of Delilah. Remember, Ahab was married to Jezebel, therefore, when a husband fell under the curse of the Ahab spirit, he initiated the Baal system in his home. This opened the door for the Jezebel spirit. Delilah seduces a man away from his home and turns him over to the enemy, but Jezebel keeps that man from returning home. She does this through fear and manipulation. Once Jezebel gives birth to Athaliah, she has completed the bulk of her assignment. Delilah cannot keep a man; her assignment is to be the bait of Satan; she has to hook that man and pull him out of God's will. After her assignment is complete, Delilah has trouble being faithful either in body or in heart. Her lovers will sense the many soul ties in her life and they will not have peace regarding her. Jezebels do hold on to their Ahabs, however, this is because Jezebel must give birth to more evil.

Ahab wasn't the first man to come in contact with what is now referred to as the Jezebel spirit; meaning he was not the first man to have what is now commonly referred to as the Ahab spirit. The first time we read about the Jezebel in operation was in the story of Adam and Eve. Sin had not yet entered mankind, even though good and evil were both present and at war. How do we know this? The tree that Adam and Eve were commanded to not eat from was called The Tree of the Knowledge of Good and Evil. God wanted mankind to remain pure; He'd already determined that the war between good and evil was not one He wanted man to enter. In other words, He was protecting us. Nevertheless, the serpent slithered into the Garden of Eden and the very first thing it did was attack the order of God; it went directly after the woman. This wasn't because she was the weaker creature; this was because Satan always tries to pervert the order of God. He did this by challenging Eve's trust in God by causing her to question God's instructions. He then tempted her with envy, telling her that she can be like God. This is the very recipe of the Jezebel spirit: distrust, religiousness, jealousy, double-mindedness and lust. Eve looked at the fruit that she was commanded not to eat and the Bible says that she "considered" it; meaning, temptation had her in its grips. She finally gave in to temptation and sin entered mankind, but it was still contained within the woman. This means that had Adam not partaken from the forbidden fruit, it is likely that God would have created another woman for Adam and He would have pronounced judgment upon Eve. He would have sent her away from the Garden and her sins would have been contained in her. Her sins would have died with her.

After her fall, Eve then tempted her husband to disobey God and eat from the tree, and he followed her lead. What happened here was that Eve was now in submission to the devil, so her first order of business was to lead her husband into sin. When Adam (God's firstborn) fell, his seed was contaminated; he became a vessel of sin who could only birth children of sin. He caused every child born to him to automatically fall. This is why we had to have the second Adam (Jesus Christ) to reconcile us to God. Undoubtedly, this was the first time we witnessed the Jezebel spirit in operation.

The Jezebel spirit entered Eve and she immediately went against the order God had established in Eden. She didn't talk with God; she immediately attempted to establish her newfound belief that both she and her husband could be like God by simply disobeying Him. In other words, Eve was trying to start what we can best describe as a new religion.

Another account of the Jezebel/ Ahab disorder is found in the story of Samson and Delilah. Samson was seduced by Delilah; we know this, but the Jezebel spirit was very much present. How so? Delilah's seduction was to captivate Samson, but her assignment was to find the source of his strength; that way, the Philistines could overcome him. This is the very nature of the Jezebel spirit. Jezebels rob men of their authority, thus allowing them to be destroyed.

When the Jezebel spirit comes into a region, church or family, it is first preceded by Ahab. Ahab is self-willed, full of ungodly ambition and most of all, fearful. Ahabs possess authority, but are too afraid to use that authority, so they pass it over to Jezebel in exchange for protection from her kingdom and whatever things they are lusting to have. Jezebels appear to be smart, strong and confident, but in truth, they draw their strength and knowledge from demons.

Women who are inhabited by Jezebel spirits oftentimes have Delilah spirits as well and will use both spirits interchangeably. Think about that one woman you know who you've witnessed in two or more romantic relationships. With one man, she was passive, seductive and obsessed. With the other man, she was dominant, deceptive and elusive. What you have witnessed is two demonic spirits in action. When the woman in question came in contact with a strong man that she could get to submit to her, she tapped into Delilah, but when she came in contact with a fearful man who she could control, she tapped into Jezebel. This is actually a very common practice by demons and it is designed to rob a man of his strength and authority by any means necessary.

When myself and my friends were on the prowl, I noticed that we all had different methods of capturing our prey. This is because we had all come from various backgrounds. Nevertheless, our methods were different, but our goals were similar: we all wanted to be loved and we wanted to be married with children. We didn't know that our hearts were wicked because we were more focused on our motives than we were on our methods. The more a woman has been "humbled" by men, the lower she will go to get what she wants. For example, one of my friends was obsessed with unavailable men (married, engaged or in a relationship). She was a very beautiful woman who could have easily gotten just about any man that she wanted, but she'd been hurt a lot. She'd been married previously and she'd also been in countless relationships, all of which had been destroyed because of infidelity. Without God, she didn't know how to get past the hurt and learn to trust again, so she became vengeful. She would do to men whatsoever they did to her. If the man she was romantically linked to had an affair, she'd have one too. She'd be pretty much public about her affair and she would make sure that the "other guy" was someone her official lover was familiar with. After a while, she became what she'd been attacked by; she became an adulteress. She loved going after unavailable men because, as she would say, "somebody did it to her first." It was hard for her to focus on her individual attackers, so she focused on women as a whole. In her eyes, women who were not friends with her were her enemies and they were all like her. In her mind, relationships were nothing but a massive cat-fight where only the strongest won. Beautiful and seductive, she used her feminine wiles to lure men to herself. She had no shame when speaking with men; she would almost immediately start talking about sex. Nevertheless, she seemed uncomfortable talking about serious issues with men. This is because she'd allowed Satan to define her worth. She saw herself as the answer to some man's problematic marriage.

One of the most promiscuous women I knew didn't look promiscuous or "easy" at all. She dressed conservatively, wasn't overly flirtatious and she didn't act extra girly with men. As a matter of fact, she wore baggy clothes, often avoided eye contact with men and could have been considered somewhat tomboyish. Nevertheless, she was shameless in her dealings. She had a live-in boyfriend, but it was as if the guy never existed.

Another friend of mine was so crafty that she'd even deceived me. I'd met her before I became a "wild-child" and she had me convinced that she was a loving, faithful and respectable young woman. I was so convinced that she was a good girl that I would often find myself loudly defending her to anyone who said otherwise. I didn't understand why her reputation was so bad and, of course, she played on my ignorance by coming to me teary-eyed every time someone said something bad about her. She knew that I believed every word that she said. I didn't find out how deceptive she was (at that time, of course) until the man she was dating (a relative of mine) opened up and started telling me about the things she'd done to him. Of course, I didn't believe him at first because she appeared to be one of those women who could do no harm to anyone. It took a lot for me to accept that my friend was a very deceptive and cunning woman. The issue that finally convinced me was when she'd unwittingly confessed to dating a guy I had been dating behind my back. Of course, she tried to recount her words, but it was too late. Years later, I ran into her again, and by that time, she wasn't hiding her heart's condition anymore. She was outright promiscuous and proud of it. With her, I learned how convincing a woman can be when she doesn't want to be discovered. Truthfully, I had never come across someone so skilled at manipulating others until I came in contact with her. We were both relatively young then and I didn't know anything about demons other than the fact that they existed and they were evil.

Again, we were all different, but we had the same destination in our view: love and marriage. This included the ones who loved to engage with married men. They'd simply come to believe that the men they were seeing were serious about commitment since they were married. They then convinced themselves that the problem lied in their wives and not the men. Because of this, they believed that they would be better wives to those guys than the wives they already had.

Please remember that there is a difference between the woman and the demon in the woman. All too often, men and women are not delivered and rehabilitated simply because people fail to distinguish them from the evil forces that drive them. After having been an immoral woman and after being surrounded by immoral women, I can truly say that most of them are nothing but victims who repeatedly respond to their pain by hurting others. Hurt people hurt people. I've found that many of the offenses we commit against one another are infectious; meaning that people often respond to their pain by hurting others in the same manner in which they've been hurt.

Devil Baiting

It's easy to look at the heart of a seductress and despise her because of the devastation she brings to individuals and families. Nevertheless, we should never forget that she has a story. Something happened to her that sent her down the wrong path. Now, this is no justification for her behavior, however, it is to get you to understand why she thinks the way she thinks. Why should we understand her? It's simple: You can never rehabilitate anyone you do not understand and you cannot understand anyone you despise.

Before I gave my life to Christ, I had been forcefully raped three times and there had been an almost successful and very violent fourth attempt. One of my rapists had been an ex-boyfriend who'd simply ignored my "no" and forced himself on me. Another rape had been

by a man I'd been romantically involved with.
The most terrifying rape I'd endured had
happened when I was only ten years old. A
neighbor had started coming to my parents'
apartment when they were at work. It had all
started when he and another neighbor were
outside our apartment one night, asking
"Jacob", a relative of mine, to tell me to come to
the window. I did and they began dancing
flirtatiously. At first, it was funny to me. I didn't
like either guy, but I did love the attention they
were giving me. After a while, both guys left
and I thought the show was over. Little did I
know, it was just beginning. One of the boys
was a thirteen-year-old boy who we will call
"Carl." Carl was in elementary school (he'd
failed a few times) and he was known for being
a bully. Many of the students were afraid of
him, including Jacob.

Carl came back to my parents' house and Jacob
let him come in. It was late in the evening and I
knew that we could get in trouble by having

someone in my parents' house while they were not home, but I didn't say anything. Carl and Jacob talked for a few minutes, and then, without warning, Carl started touching me. I told him to stop and that's when it happened. Carl picked me up over his shoulders and carried me to my bedroom. I screamed and tried to fight my way to freedom, but he was much bigger and much stronger than me. Jacob followed us in the bedroom and watched as Carl threw me on my bed. I remember that I was wearing my favorite dress and some white stockings.

Carl was violent and angry. He started forcefully removing my clothes and covering my mouth with his hand. I cried and screamed, and that's when I realized that Jacob was hovering over me, holding my hands down. I threatened to tell on Jacob, but no words would suffice. I laid there crying as he raped me for the first time.

Carl would go on to rape me a few more times before I told my parents. One of the most terrifying times was when I'd looked out the window and saw him coming. I remember how angry he looked as he approached the front door of my parents' apartment. I had become terrified of him and Jacob made sure that he quieted me by telling me that if I told my parents, they were going to whoop me for letting Carl come in the first time. I told him that I hadn't let him come in; he did, but he recanted with, "We let him in, so if you tell, you will get a whooping too."

When Carl came into the house, I had already run into my parents' bedroom and hid underneath the bed. At ten years old, I was a lot smaller than most girls my age. I was almost always mistaken for a six or seven-year-old. Because my frame was small, I was able to fit underneath the bed, but neither Jacob nor Carl could get under it. Carl stayed at the side of the bed near the entrance to my parents' room and Jacob went to the other side of the bed. Both boys kept reaching for my leg, but they couldn't reach me. Finally, Jacob went out of the room and emerged with a broom. He took the handle of the broom and began to jab me with it. I discovered that day how limited one's movement is under a bed. I couldn't move my hands fast enough to prevent Jacob from jabbing my rib cage. He would threaten my face with the broom and when I would move my hands upward to protect my face, he would use that moment to shove the broom handle into my side. The pain was unbearable, so I started scooting out of the broom's reach, unaware of the fact that I was moving closer and closer to Carl. Suddenly, I felt a hand on my ankle and I felt myself being pulled from under the bed.

Carl was furious that he had to work so hard to get me from under the bed, so he threw me on my parents' bed and that rape was more violent than the first two rapes. I was terrified of him, but I was also terrified of telling my parents. When I finally did tell my parents, like Jacob had warned, I was whooped because they felt I'd brought the rape on myself. Honestly, I can say now that they simply didn't know any better at that time.

Next, when I was twelve years old, one of my dad's friends decided that he didn't want to play "uncle" to me anymore. He wanted much more.

"Ramsey" was well past forty years old and I'd known him all of my life. He was probably at the hospital the day I was born. Nevertheless, that didn't stop him from pursuing me. He would often follow me to the kitchen or anywhere I went and he'd began to fondle me. I was afraid because he was truly like an uncle to me and I didn't want to upset him, but at the same time, I didn't like his advances. So, I tried my best to avoid him at all costs, but he was pretty much at my parents' house every day and he'd wait for any opportunity he could get to fondle me.

Ramsey never got a chance to have sex with me. *Catching me in a room while my parents were in another room didn't give him enough time to satisfy his lusts, so he settled for fondling me or molesting me with his hands.* To keep me quiet, he would give me money or have me ironing his clothes so he could justify giving me money.

I hated every minute of Ramsey's visits and the money he gave me definitely didn't make the pain go away, so I tried to find a way to tell my parents what he had been doing. I finally got this opportunity when I was fourteen years old. Ramsey called my parents' house and asked for my dad. "He's not home yet, but he'll be here soon," I answered. I hoped that he'd get off the line, but he didn't. "Is your Mom home?" he asked. Of course, she wasn't home either. That's when he started telling me about a property he had that my parents knew nothing about. He told me that I was mature for my age, he was very attracted to me and he didn't feel that my parents understood my needs. He asked me to meet him at the corner market in twenty minutes. "Don't bring anything ... no clothes, nothing. I'll buy you new clothes and I'll teach you how to drive," he said. He tried to offer me everything that a young woman would want, including not ever having to return to school, but I wasn't attracted to him; plus, I feared my parents. He was far too old for me and I honestly saw him as an uncle. To me, what he was doing was incestuous ... it was gross.

When Ramsey asked me to meet him at the corner market, I panicked. I'd mastered avoiding him ... especially being alone with him, but this was a new level of scary for me. I didn't know what to do, but I did know that I wasn't going to run away with Ramsey. The most reoccurring thought I had was "What if he gets me and hides me at his place? What will happen if the police start looking for me and they start closing in on him?" I was young, but I was far from stupid. My immediate thoughts were that I'd end up buried in his backyard. That was enough to scare me into telling my parents.

When my parents came home, I told them everything. I was pacing and crying because of how terrified I was. My dad went to the phone and called Ramsey and, of course, he started lying. I rushed to my room in fear and began to pace. I didn't want to hear his voice and I couldn't bear anyone looking at me. My mom came into the room a few minutes later and said that Ramsey had told them that he was just joking around with me. When I looked at her face, I knew that she was basically trying to get both sides of the story. Pain gripped my soul and my anguish was evident. I told her what he'd been doing to me for the last two years and I tried to, in a sense, make my case. My mom said okay before closing my bedroom door and returning to the living room. I don't remember much else about that night, but I do remember that it was one of the most terrifying nights of my life.

The next day when I returned home from school, Ramsey was sitting in the living room. I remember opening the door and freezing when I saw him. After the shock faded, I rushed to my room. My dad followed me into the room and explained that Ramsey had told him that he was just joking around with me; plus, he'd been threatening to kill himself. He said that this was the reason why he'd let him come over. I can remember telling my dad something to the effect of, "Most dads would have volunteered to do it for him! He wouldn't have to kill himself!" But that didn't change anything. Ramsey continued to visit my parents' house. To pay me back for telling on him, he'd greet my sister and brother, but he wouldn't greet me. I didn't care about him not greeting me, but I didn't like being picked on. He'd also give my siblings

money, but wouldn't say a word to me or give
me anything. He did slow down with visiting
my parents and when I turned 16, my parents
were divorced. Most children are sad when
their parents divorce, but I wasn't. I knew that
without my dad around, I wouldn't have to see
Ramsey anymore, so I threw a party when my
parents separated.

As you can see, Satan was sending a clear
message to me. He was telling me that he
could do anything he wanted to me and I could
cry for help, but no one would help me; no one
would protect me. I received that message
loud and clear and I began to develop a violent
heart towards men. I was honestly developing
the heart of a seductive murderer. Satan lured
me in and started using my pain, fear and lack
of a proper covering to disciple me into his
kingdom.

Another rape attempt had occurred when I
was nineteen and it was from a man who I

hadn't been romantically involved with. I'd placed him in the infamous "friend zone" for a year or two, even though I knew he liked me.

"Gregory" was in the military full-time, so I rarely got to see him since he worked and lived overseas. He was a relatively handsome man, but for whatever reason, he wasn't my "type." In other words, the demons that were in me were not interested in him. Plus, to me, Gregory's motives were obvious. He wanted sex and I saw that. As a matter of fact, I can honestly say that he'd reminded me of the men who'd molested me in my past. At that stage in my life, I didn't like men to touch me. If sex was initiated, I had to be the one who initiated it. I didn't realize why I was like that at that time, but looking back, I can say that it was because of what I'd gone through as a child.

When Gregory called me, I was engaged to be married to another guy. I hadn't heard from Gregory for anywhere between six months to a year because he had been overseas. I was at work when Gregory called me and told me he was in town. Because I knew that he liked me, I told him that I was engaged and that I couldn't see him, but Gregory was insistent. He reminded me that we were friends and then, he told me that he'd brought me some jewelry back from overseas. I was young and materialistic back then, so the idea of getting new jewelry (especially from overseas) was exciting for me. I told myself that I'd go to Gregory's house, talk with him for a few minutes, collect my new jewelry and leave. I didn't realize that there was no new jewelry. Just like Satan does to us, Gregory used something he knew I wanted to lure me.

When I arrived at Gregory's house, I saw two young ladies sitting on the dining room floor, smoking marijuana. I had never smoked marijuana and I hated the smell of it, so when Gregory suggested that we go to his room, I quickly agreed. I didn't want the smell of the

drugs to get into my clothes, so I followed
Gregory into his room, telling myself that I
wasn't going to let him close the door. I was
overly determined to remain faithful to my
fiancé.

As soon as we entered the room, Gregory tried
to close the door, but I threw my leg in the way
and stopped him. Gregory laughed at me and I
thought all was well. A man making advances
was not an alarm for me; it was pretty much
expected, but I reasoned within myself that I'd
reject his advances and get what I came there
to get. Gregory tried to close the door again,
and just like the first time, I put my leg in the
way and began to tell him to stop trying to
close the door. It all happened very fast.
Gregory picked me up, closed the bedroom
door and fell onto the bed on top of me. At
first, I thought he was playing, but this didn't
change the fact that I was angry. So, I began
to curse at him. When I looked into his eyes, I
realized that he wasn't playing. I saw darkness

in his eyes. I saw death in his eyes. Terror
gripped me, but my anger overrode my terror
temporarily. At first, I kept cursing at Gregory
and telling him to get off me, but when he
started choking me and screaming at me to
"shut up," I realized that my life was in danger.

Gregory attacked me for no less than thirty
minutes, but as scared as I was, I was
determined not to be raped. He would choke
me until I felt weak, and once he felt like I
couldn't resist anymore, he'd proceed to trying
to take off my clothes. Nevertheless, I kept
fighting, crying and begging. In the end,
Gregory did finally get my jeans off me, but by
that time, he was so drained from the fight that
he couldn't do anything. I was around ninety
pounds (no more than a hundred pounds) and
Gregory was over six feet tall and full of solid
muscle. It didn't matter though. I was more
determined to not get raped than he was to
rape me. At the same time, I now know that
God protected me.

I didn't call the police and report the incident because I was afraid that they'd blame me for my assault. I imagined myself in court being emotionally raped by a jury who wanted to know why I'd gone to Gregory's bedroom in the first place. I had never experienced anyone trying to defend me before, so I can honestly say now that I understand why I was so afraid to call the police.

As you can see, the enemy began to "disciple" me at a young age. He attacked me so much in my youth that I was ashamed to tell people what I'd gone through. Most of my close friends knew, but I was pretty mum about my experiences with everyone else. I'd been molested countless times, so I saw myself as a sexual creature. I'd been molested by family members, so I saw myself as a dirty creature. That was the message Satan was trying to convey to me. Each attack created an even greater void in me, coupled with a greater and even more desperate desire to be loved and protected. Satan then used those voids to lead me further into darkness. At the same time, every one of those attacks that occurred in my youth became individual blotches on my soul that I wanted to wash away. I wanted to cleanse myself of my past, so I used voluntary sex as a method of cleansing myself from the things that had happened against my will (or when I was too young to understand what I was doing). This is the strategic demoralization of women. Satan tears women down so that he can build them back up the way he wants them to be.

Always remember this: A woman is first torn down in order for a seductress to be built up. Satan likes to attack women sexually and he often starts when they are young. The National Center for Victims of Crime reported that one out of every five girls is a victim of sexual abuse. Of course, their findings are based on the number of reported cases. The truth is that most cases go unreported. As a victim of sexual abuse, I estimate that one out of every three women have been the victim of sexual abuse, but of course, I can't back those findings (and neither can they). The majority of the women I've met have been sexually abused or assaulted at some point in their lives (mostly by family members). Some women reported the abuse, but most did not.

The main reason that women don't report sexual abuse is because the person preying on them is usually a loved one (uncle, brother, family friend, etc.). I've even met a few women who'd been raped or molested by their biological fathers. No one can imagine the devastation that such a crime brings, especially when the perpetrator is related to the victim. Additionally, people see the response from the woman through poor choices, but they do not know what she's responding to.

Some women respond by becoming promiscuous; some respond by entering same-sex unions, and some respond by committing suicide. The reason for this is that it tears a woman's image into shreds and confuses her altogether. After being raped or molested, a woman's body means little to nothing to her because, in most cases, she won't feel connected to it anymore. (During the course of a rape, fondling or assault, a woman will oftentimes mentally disconnect herself from her body.) She won't feel connected to her body and all too often, sexual abuse makes women regret being women. They begin to see their body parts as magnets for monsters and objects that bring out the worst in people. The more abuse she sustains, the less connected she will be to her body. Now, this doesn't mean that she will get to a point where she isn't affected by sexual abuse or that she'll be okay with someone molesting or raping her. Additionally, it doesn't mean that she doesn't care what happens to her (because she will). Instead, what it means is that she becomes conflicted within herself. On one hand, she has trouble mentally separating herself from her body, but on the other hand, she will find herself rejecting her body. Because of this, she will likely respond to sexual abuse by:

1. **Becoming promiscuous**- Promiscuity is oftentimes a woman's attempt to wash away the people who've violated her. This isn't so much as trying to wash the perpetrators away physically as it is mentally. She is oftentimes tormented by the thoughts of what happened to her and, at the same time, she is repeatedly reminded of how low she felt the moment it happened or immediately after it was done. Additionally, promiscuity is her way of responding to having her choice taken away from her by the person or people who assaulted her. Being able to finally choose if she wants to have sex, who she wants to have sex with, and when she wants to have sex is empowering and addictive.

2. **Becoming a workaholic or a busy**

body- Victims of sexual abuse are oftentimes tormented by the memories of the abuse they suffered. For this reason, many women will become over-achievers, tossing themselves into numerous extracurricular activities at school or working several jobs. They don't like to be idle because it gives the devil too much time to torment them. At the same time, many become busy bodies (gossips) because this allows them to focus on the issues, problems and downfalls of others, rather than being reminded and tormented by their own demons. Either way, many women who've been sexually assaulted will find some way to busy themselves.

3. **Becoming very competitive towards others, especially other women-** Sexual abuse victims often feel inferior to their peers and because of this, they will oftentimes be overly competitive or repeatedly compare themselves to

others. This opens up the door for her
to become an adulteress.

4. **Practicing poor hygiene**- This mainly
happens when the woman lives in the
house with her rapist. Some women will
intentionally try to make themselves
physically unappealing to their rapists by
practicing poor hygiene.

5. **Excessive partying and substance
abuse**- A woman who has been
sexually abused and has not had any
form of counseling or deliverance will
oftentimes turn to drugs and alcohol in
her attempt to "treat" her pain.
Intoxication allows her to temporarily
escape her tormented mind and simply
enjoy the moment she's in; that is, of
course, if she's not an angry drunk.

6. **Surrounding self with bad company**-
Victims of sexual abuse oftentimes look
for ways to belong to a group. Of
course, we have a natural need to
belong, but victims of sexual abuse will

oftentimes ally themselves with others who are rejected, tormented and abused. They will oftentimes ally themselves with rebels and people they feel can and will protect them.

7. **Dressing and/or behaving like a man-** This is another attempt by a victim to "turn off" the person who's been preying on her.

8. **Avoiding any sport or activity that appears to be "girly"-** Some victims of sexual abuse will get involved in high-activity sports like basketball, football and soccer. They will often avoid joining any activity that draws attention to their femininity like becoming a cheerleader or a majorette.

9. **Joining every sport that appears to be "girly"-** There are some victims who want to disassociate themselves from their gender (at least in the eyes of their abusers or potential abusers), but then again, some women respond to abuse

by becoming "extra girly." Many will become cheerleaders, dancers or majorettes in an attempt to rebuild their self-worth and thrust themselves into the public eye. The reason for wanting to be in the public eye is to not only feel human again, but it is also to send a message to their abusers that they are not afraid to go before an audience. Now, of course, this isn't to say that every "girl" or "not-so-girly" woman is the victim of sexual abuse, but it is to bring attention to the fact that it is present.

10. **Isolating herself from others (especially men)**- Victims of sexual abuse are often tormented by the fear of being raped, molested or assaulted again. For this reason, many women isolate themselves from their loved ones and peers.

11. **Surrounding herself with others (especially men):** Have you ever heard

a woman boast about having a lot of
male friends? If so, it's likely that she
has been raped or molested.
Surrounding herself with people
(especially men) helps the victim to feel
protected.

12. **Making poor choices**- Sometimes, a
victim's choices is nothing but her cry for
help.

Of course, these are not the only signs of
sexual abuse; there are many more, but the
ones listed above are some of the most
obvious.

Most seductresses are victims of sexual abuse;
they were created in pain. There are some
who were never sexually abused, but they
were physically, verbally, emotionally or
financially abused. Again, their choice to be
promiscuous is oftentimes a response to what
they've been through and the belief systems
they've developed in their pain. Their
promiscuity is almost always their own

attempts to overcome their devils. Below, you will see how victims of each form of abuse, outside of sexual abuse, respond to their pain.

Physical Abuse- Victims of physical abuse are oftentimes found in long-standing relationships where abuse is prevalent. They are usually found linked to sexually promiscuous men and they respond to their lovers' promiscuity by being promiscuous. This intensifies the physical abuse they are enduring at home and most of the people who know them passionately believe that if they are to escape their abusive lovers that their lives (and choices) will be better. Eventually, they do end their relationships with their violent lovers only to find themselves in the arms of another well-disguised abuser.

Verbal Abuse- Victims of verbal abuse are oftentimes going from one relationship to the next in search of kind words. They will oftentimes be found in medium to long-standing relationships, but their relationships almost always end because of words spoken. Additionally, they are oftentimes unfaithful because they are easily swayed by words. For example, a woman who has been told by her mother that she will never amount to anything will likely find herself in relationships with men who are just as vicious with their words as her mother was. In each relationship, she will endure a lot of verbal abuse and, in most cases, she'll come to believe what has been said about her. When she comes across another man who speaks kindly to her, she will be easily flattered by him and will oftentimes respond by sleeping with him and entering a relationship with him. These relationships usually end when the new guy is no longer the new guy. It happens when he becomes the "main guy" and has gotten so accustomed to speaking word curses over her that he fails to notice the signs that another guy has entered the picture and said something nice to his lover.

Emotional Abuse- Much like verbal abuse, emotional abuse is oftentimes the result of spoken words. With emotional abuse, the victim is manipulated emotionally by someone they love. Basically, the people who have abused them have learned to use their love for them or their fear of losing them as tools to control them. For example, a mother who uses her old age and poor health to get her daughter to do whatever she wants her to do. Before she had health issues, she would buy things for her daughter and help her out whenever she needed help, but everything she did for her was not done in love. It was her way of buying her right to control her. These are oftentimes Jezebel - Ahab relationships, whereas, in this example, the mother has what is commonly referred to as a Jezebel spirit and she has "ahab'ed" her daughter.

Victims of emotional abuse are oftentimes promiscuous simply because it is hard for them to find men who are willing to commit to them.

Nevertheless, they want to be loved so they often try to manipulate their way into the hearts of their lovers or their potential lovers. This rarely works and when it does work, the effects of their witchcraft are short-lived. The reason for this is they will oftentimes find themselves in relationships with men who are just as controlling and manipulative as their mothers, and a power struggle will ensue. The man will win for a few months; maybe even a few years, but eventually, what is in her mother will win out because the mother is skilled at manipulating her.

Financial Abuse: This form of abuse is more common than most people are aware of. With financial abuse, one authority (oftentimes a parent) will use money to control the person or people he or she has authority over. Much like emotional abuse, this is usually another common tactic of the Jezebel spirit.
Victims of financial abuse are oftentimes expected by their parents to take a certain path

in life, but they rarely do. The parents will verbally and emotionally abuse them in an attempt to get them to become financially independent of them, but at the same time, the parents will continue to make them financially dependent on them. This creates an unhealthy co-dependency between the parents and the child or children. The parents fear that if their child or children were to become financially independent, they won't need them anymore. So, they become conflicted and begin to send mixed messages to their children. They will criticize them for not living up to their expectations, but they won't allow their children to learn the value of working for what they want and need. So, for example, a mother who financially abuses her daughter will tell her to quit her job the very moment she complains about being questioned, rebuked or criticized by her superiors or co-workers. She will say things like, "You don't need to work under those conditions! You got your mom and I will take care of you!"

Like victims of emotional abuse, victims of financial abuse will oftentimes find themselves in an inordinate love triangle between their controlling parents and their lovers. This almost always leads to promiscuity because these victims have trouble holding on to men.

Again, seductresses are created in pain and their pain leads them to make some really poor choices in life. Satan loves to inflict pain on people because pain is like an infectious disease; the carriers of it will repeatedly transfer it to others until they themselves are cured of it. All too often, victims of abuse repeatedly birth out pain because pain is what they carry. They don't reason like what most would consider "normal" people because they were not brought up in "normal" conditions. For example, before God saved and changed me, I hurt others because I was hurting. Sadly enough, I didn't realize that I was in pain because, like most victims of sexual abuse, I'd learned to function in my dysfunction. My abnormal life was normal to me. I surrounded myself with women who were like me ... women who were functionally dysfunctional. We didn't realize it then, but we were comparing and sharing the mentalities (and demons) we'd picked up in our pain. Even though we were similar in many ways, we didn't always reason the same because we had all been brought up in different conditions. For example, before I met my old friends, I had never been involved with a married man. I had a personal (passionate) hatred for married men who cheated on their wives and I was very vocal about that. As a matter of fact, I remember being at a club with a friend of mine one night when a familiar face walked in. I had seen the guy hanging out at my beautician's house, but I didn't know him personally. I knew that he was around my age and that my beautician referred to him as her son, even though they weren't related. He was a handsome guy, but the minute my beautician said he was married, my interest in him fizzled.

At the club that night, the guy appeared to be somewhat intoxicated, but I could tell that he was still in his right mind, for the most part. When I saw him heading my way, I smiled at him because I knew him, but inwardly, I was fuming. I recognized that oh-too-familiar lustful look in his eyes. I'd seen it many times before (from other men) and before he'd approached me, he was one of the few men that I'd had respect for.

He leaned in and whispered in my ear and I couldn't believe what I was hearing. As a matter of fact, I had him to repeat himself several times before I could respond. He offered to give me five hundred dollars to sleep with him. Again, I was in denial; I didn't realize that I was promiscuous. I compared myself to other promiscuous women (outside of my friends) and I thought I was a rare and decent woman. I thought I was a woman living a normal life and dealing with a few normal and not-so-normal issues. I didn't exchange sex for money and I was infuriated that he felt comfortable approaching me and making such a degrading proposition; plus, he was a married man. This only further angered me. I don't remember the intensity of my response, but I do remember him trying to calm me down. The fact is ... I was promiscuous, but the devil deceived me into believing that I was a moral woman because I only had sex when I was considered some man's (exclusive) girlfriend. His approach, while offensive, represented what he saw in me. I wasn't a standard, stand-on-the-street-corner prostitute, but the truth was, like most women, I was exchanging sex for love and this is a form of prostitution. The only difference between me and a street prostitute was that they were honest with themselves about what they were. My "boyfriends" were nothing but "Johns" who pretended to love me to get what they wanted from me. This was how they paid for sex. Of course, there were some who thought they loved me so they were just as deceived as I was. My friends, for the most part, were more honest with themselves than I was with myself. Denial was my coping mechanism.

Some of my friends, on the other hand, didn't mind sleeping with married men, and of course, a couple of them thought I was crazy for turning down his offer. The point is ... we were all sexually immoral, but we had our own individual beliefs and our own personal demons. It goes without saying that after hanging around them for a while, I ended up playing the mistress to a married man (and they picked up some of the demons I had as well), but because of my beliefs and my disdain for two-timing men, I could not stay in that relationship long. I had been the other woman in one or two relationships where the couples weren't married prior to that, but every time I involved myself with an unavailable man, I could never take him seriously.

Another way that the spirit behind sexual

immorality enters a woman is through the absence of her father or a godly father-figure. Consider the biblical days. Nations would go to war with one another and the nation that was victorious would often kill off the men and take their wives and daughters into captivity. Without the protection of a father or husband, the women would have no choice but to give in to the lusts and desires of their captors. Amazingly enough, Satan still practices this war-tactic, but these days, the war is in the realm of the spirit and the warriors aren't always men. (Of course, child —wife slavery still exists today.)

Again, some of Satan's most effective weapons are women. He loves to use women to break up the family unit. He uses women to bring men into lustful captivity and the worst part is ... those who are taken captive by the lustful snares of an adulteress don't even realize that they are prisoners (and tools) of warfare!

When the family is broken up, Satan will then use the pain he's inflicted on the estranged wife to get her to enter sexual immorality. He will also use his newfound access to her daughters to pervert them and cause them not to trust men. He's doing the very same thing nations would do when they took the women from other nations into captivity; he is raping the women, but this time, he does it mentally, emotionally, spiritually and financially.

The women who come from broken homes have to struggle to re-establish their trust in men and all too often, many never recover because the most influential men in their lives (their fathers) hadn't loved them enough to stick around and protect them. Instead, they were led astray by their own selfishness, pride and sense of entitlement. Remember, the very definition of "seduce" is to "lead astray." Basically, what Satan does is "fish" men out of their homes using the seductress as bait. This, of course, is to destroy them, bring shame to their names (a good name is a blessing from God) and to open their families for demonic attack. Whereas for men who aren't married, Satan uses seductresses to keep them from finding their "good thing from the Lord" and obtaining favor from God. This is one of the reasons God warns us to not be led by our flesh.

Galatians 5:16-24 (ESV): But I say, walk by the Spirit, and you will not gratify the desires of the flesh. For the desires of the flesh are against the Spirit, and the desires of the Spirit are against the flesh, for these are opposed to each other, to keep you from doing the things you want to do. But if you are led by the Spirit, you are not under the law. Now the works of the flesh are evident: sexual immorality, impurity, sensuality, idolatry, sorcery, enmity, strife, jealousy, fits of anger, rivalries, dissensions, divisions, envy, drunkenness, orgies, and things like these. I warn you, as I warned you before, that those who do such things will not inherit the kingdom of God. But the fruit of the Spirit is love, joy, peace, patience, kindness, goodness, faithfulness, gentleness, self-control; against such things there is no law. And those who belong to Christ Jesus have crucified the flesh with its passions and desires.

An immoral woman is a weapon formed against the men who love her and the men who lie with her, but before she became a weapon, she was disciplined by the devil through a series of painful events. In other words, Satan made a disciple of darkness out of her by tossing her into darkness and starving her of love, wisdom, knowledge and understanding. It took a lot of pain to break her and it took a lot of deception to convince her to take the path that she's taken. Nevertheless, Satan has the perfect recipe to turn a woman into an immoral woman. The amount of pain he inflicts on a woman is determined by how deep he wants her to go into the depths of darkness.

The Trap is Set

To better understand the power of a seductive woman, we must first examine the story of Samson and Delilah.

Judges 16:1-22 (ESV): Samson went to Gaza, and there he saw a prostitute, and he went in to her. The Gazites were told, "Samson has come here." And they surrounded the place and set an ambush for him all night at the gate of the city. They kept quiet all night, saying, "Let us wait till the light of the morning; then we will kill him." But Samson lay till midnight, and at midnight he arose and took hold of the doors of the gate of the city and the two posts, and pulled them up, bar and all, and put them on his shoulders and carried them to the top of the hill that is in front of Hebron.

After this he loved a woman in the Valley of Sorek, whose name was Delilah. And the lords of the Philistines came up to her and said to her, "<u>Seduce</u> him, and see where his great strength lies, and by what means we may overpower him, that we may bind him to humble him. And we will each give you 1,100 pieces of silver." So Delilah said to Samson, "Please tell me where your great strength lies, and how you might be bound, that one could subdue you."

Samson said to her, "If they bind me with seven fresh bowstrings that have not been dried, then I shall become weak and be like any other man." Then the lords of the Philistines brought up to her seven fresh bowstrings that had not been dried, and she bound him with them. Now she had men lying in ambush in an inner chamber. And she said to him, "The Philistines are upon you, Samson!" But he snapped the bowstrings, as a thread of flax snaps when it touches the fire. So the secret of his strength was not known.

Then Delilah said to Samson, "Behold, you have mocked me and told me lies. Please tell me how you might be bound." And he said to her, "If

they bind me with new ropes that have not
been used, then I shall become weak and be
like any other man." So Delilah took new ropes
and bound him with them and said to him, "The
Philistines are upon you, Samson!" And the men
lying in ambush were in an inner chamber. But
he snapped the ropes off his arms like a
thread.

Then Delilah said to Samson, "Until now you
have mocked me and told me lies. Tell me how
you might be bound." And he said to her, "If you
weave the seven locks of my head with the
web and fasten it tight with the pin, then I shall
become weak and be like any other man." So
while he slept, Delilah took the seven locks of
his head and wove them into the web. And she
made them tight with the pin and said to him,
"The Philistines are upon you, Samson!" But he
awoke from his sleep and pulled away the pin,
the loom, and the web.

And she said to him, "How can you say, 'I love
you,' when your heart is not with me? You
have mocked me these three times, and you

have not told me where your great strength lies." <u>And when she pressed him hard with her words day after day, and urged him, his soul was vexed to death.</u> And he told her all his heart, and said to her, "A razor has never come upon my head, for I have been a Nazirite to God from my mother's womb. If my head is shaved, then my strength will leave me, and I shall become weak and be like any other man." When Delilah saw that he had told her all his heart, she sent and called the lords of the Philistines, saying, "Come up again, for he has told me all his heart." Then the lords of the Philistines came up to her and brought the money in their hands. She made him sleep on her knees. And she called a man and had him shave off the seven locks of his head. Then she began to torment him, and his strength left him. And she said, "The Philistines are upon you, Samson!" And he awoke from his sleep and said, "I will go out as at other times and shake myself free." But he did not know that the Lord had left him. And the Philistines seized him and gouged out his eyes and brought him down to Gaza and bound him with bronze shackles.

As we can see here, Delilah was a seductress; she was a woman who used her words to get what she wanted. That is the power of seduction. Most people think seduction, for example, incorporates a woman dancing seductively in front of a man, but this is only a small part of seduction. Think of it this way ... a seductress is a demonically trained assassin, assigned to lure a man to his death. His death isn't just his natural death, but it is the destruction of his career, his family and his good name. She will bring a man to utter ruins, but she appears to be as harmless as a dove; this is why she is one of Satan's most effective weapons.

God said in Proverbs 18:22 that, "He who finds a wife finds a good thing and obtains favor from the LORD." A wife is favor and Satan knows this. A wife is called a help meet; she is

assigned to help her husband with his purpose.
She is custom designed favor. A seductress,
on the other hand, is Satan's attempt to stop,
hinder and destroy what God has set in motion.
She is judgment manifested in the flesh. She is,
without question, a demonic assassin and
many men have succumb to her wiles.

We've all heard that a woman is like a delicate
flower and this can be true for both good and
bad women, but a flower isn't always safe. For
example, there is an insect called an "ambush
bug" that hides on flowers, waiting to capture
any insect that lands on that flower. Many
ambush bugs are perfectly colored to blend in
with the flowers they hide themselves on.
According to popsci.com, *flowers attract
insects with movement. Flowers are known to
attract pollinating insects through a variety of
means, from alluring fragrances and nectar to
vibrant colors and shapes.* This means that
flowers are naturally attractive to pollinating
insects. This also means that the ambush bug,

also known as the assassin bug, uses the seductive power of the flower to lure its prey. Once the prey lands on the flower, the ambush bug mimics natural elements like wind in order to sneak up on the unsuspecting prey. Without warning, it pierces the insect and injects a paralyzing venom into it. The insect is then paralyzed, but it is very much alive. The ambush bug then begins to eat the insect alive.

This bug is very similar to a seductive woman. Satan understands that men are naturally attracted to women, so he uses a seductive woman as his camouflage. The smells of her perfume, the curve of her body and the sweet and sensual sound of her voice are powerful enough to lure men. When an unsuspecting man goes after her, Satan will use the sound of her voice to get her to mimic favor. Once a man opens his heart or lies down with such a woman, he is suddenly ambushed by the enemy. Even though he is very much alive, Satan begins to paralyze him, starting with his purpose, his finances, his mind and his health. Over the years, even after he's gotten away from that woman, Satan continues to suck the life out of him; that is, unless he gets saved, sanctified, filled with the Holy Spirit and delivered.

The word "seductress" comes from the word "seduce" and it simply means to "lead astray". Of course, anytime you see the suffix "tress", it is a feminine reference; meaning a seductress is a woman who leads others astray. Ironically enough, Hollywood has seduced many into believing that a seductress is a beautiful, sexually adventurous (and harmless) woman. She is portrayed as favor, but this is very far from the truth. She is not favor; she is a curse.

The Delilah seductress is oftentimes portrayed as submissive; sometimes, even child-like, playful, loving, and highly misunderstood. The Jezebel seductress is oftentimes portrayed as a dominant, sadomasochistic woman who loves to mix pain with pleasure. Of course, every man who is entertained by this will be attracted to the woman who has the spirit that matches the spirit he is bound by. Some will be attracted to the Delilah, whereas, others will be attracted to the Jezebel. I've found that men who tend to like Delilahs are oftentimes successful (or at least, they think they're successful), proud and somewhat controlling. They love being the head of their homes and the life of the party. They love being the envy of their friends. On the other hand, men who tend to like Jezebels are oftentimes passive, fearful and unsure of themselves. They have what we call "mommy issues." Jezebels usually take on a motherly role with such men and because of this, men who like Jezebels usually turn over their responsibilities (and their wages) to their new slave-masters.

A seductress can use her words, body and influence to seduce people to do what she wants them to do, but a seductress's most powerful weapon is not her form; it is her words.

Proverbs 7:1-23 (ESV): My son, keep my words and treasure up my commandments with you; keep my commandments and live; keep my teaching as the apple of your eye; bind them on your fingers; write them on the tablet of your heart. Say to wisdom, "You are my sister," and call insight your intimate friend, to keep you from the forbidden woman, from the adulteress with her smooth words. For at the window of my house I have looked out through my lattice, and I have seen among the simple, I have perceived among the youths, a young man lacking sense, passing along the street near her corner, taking the road to her house in the twilight, in the evening, at the time of night and darkness. And behold, the woman meets him, dressed as a prostitute, wily of heart. She is loud and wayward; her feet do not stay at home; now in the street, now in the market, and at every corner she lies in wait. She seizes him and kisses him, and with bold face she says to him, "I had to offer sacrifices, and today I have paid my vows; so now I have come out to meet you, to seek you eagerly, and I have found you. I have spread my couch with coverings, colored linens from Egyptian linen; I have perfumed my bed with myrrh, aloes, and cinnamon. Come, let us take our fill of love till morning; let us delight ourselves with love. For my husband is not at home; he has gone on a long journey; he took a bag of money with him; at full moon he will come home." With much seductive speech she persuades him; with her smooth talk she compels him. All at once he follows her, as an ox goes to the slaughter, or as a stag is caught fast till an arrow pierces its liver; as a bird rushes into a snare; he does not know that it will cost him his life.

Proverbs 5:1-14 (ESV): My son, be attentive to my wisdom; incline your ear to my understanding, that you may keep discretion, and your lips may guard knowledge. For the lips of a forbidden woman drip honey, and her speech is smoother than oil, but in the end she is bitter as wormwood, sharp as a two-edged sword. Her feet go down to death; her steps follow the path to Sheol; she does not ponder the path of life; her ways wander, and she does not know it. And now, O sons, listen to me, and do not depart from the words of my mouth. Keep your way far from her, and do not go near the door of her house, lest you give your honor to others and your years to the merciless, lest strangers take their fill of your strength, and your labors go to the house of a foreigner, and at the end of your life you groan, when your flesh and body are consumed, and you say, "How I hated discipline, and my heart despised reproof! I did not listen to the voice of my teachers or incline my ear to my instructors. I am at the brink of utter ruin in the assembled congregation."

A seductress is an open pit; her assignment is to cause the fall of great and renown men. She is death's bait.

Proverbs 2:16-19 (ESV): So you will be delivered from the forbidden woman, from the adulteress with her smooth words, who forsakes the companion of her youth and forgets the covenant of her God; for her house sinks down to death, and her paths to the departed; none who go to her come back, nor do they regain the paths of life.

A seductress's assignment is to reduce a man, meaning, she is to lower him. A better way to say this is...she is designed to make a man edible for the enemy.

1 Peter 5:8 (ESV): Be sober-minded; be watchful. Your adversary the devil prowls around like a roaring lion, seeking someone to devour.

Proverbs 6:26 (KJV): For by means of a whorish woman a man is brought to a piece of bread: and the adulteress will hunt for the precious life.

A seductress is also designed to stop small

men who are called to greatness from reaching their potential. They give men the illusion that they are going somewhere, all the while, keeping them immobilized in the spiritual realm. At the same time, when a great and renown man falls into the trap of an immoral woman, Satan uses that man's platform to promote his kingdom. This is why we see great men of God be promoted by God, only to leave their wives and pursue immoral women. God wanted to use those men to promote His kingdom and to promote godly marriages, but Satan found sin in them and tempted them outside the will of God. From there, he caused them to reject their favor (wives) because Satan knows that the wife is the main reason that God elevated that man in the first place. Without his wife, he cannot and will not sustain his position in greatness. For this reason, Satan will use that man's platform to promote pride, adultery and a host of demonic spirits. Without warning, he will strike these men down so that he can publicly broadcast their falls.

Why would Satan want to promote their falls?
Because they are representatives of the living
God. Even in their sin, they are verbally
promoting the Kingdom of God and Satan's goal
is to discredit the gospel. It doesn't matter
what era you're in, all you have to do is
conduct a Google search and you will find some
well-known man of God who has left his wife
and gotten with an immoral woman. Little does
he know that the platform God has placed him
on is the very same platform Satan is using him
to promote his adultery on. Additionally, it is
the very same platform that, should he not
repent, he will fall on. To repent means to
humble oneself and turn back to the path of
God. It is to admit one's error, renounce one's
sins and return to the path of God. It also
means to get out of Satan's reach.
Nevertheless, it is very difficult for a man who
has been elevated to acknowledge his faults
because pride is strongest when it bears the
weight of the public eye. For this reason, many
men who fall into the trap of the seductress will

stiffen their necks when rebuked.

Proverbs 16:18 (ESV): Pride goes before destruction, and a haughty spirit before a fall.

Most seductresses are not aware of their demonic assignments. They simply know that there is something they want and they believe that the men in their sights can help them to get it. At the same time, a seductress is crafty; she knows what to do and say to get what she wants. She even knows the tone that she should use to get it.

Proverbs 7:24-27 (ESV): And now, O sons, listen to me, and be attentive to the words of my mouth. Let not your heart turn aside to her ways; do not stray into her paths, for many a victim has she laid low, and all her slain are a mighty throng. Her house is the way to Sheol, going down to the chambers of death.

A seductress may appear to be naive and may even have flunked out of school, but her intellect is not a representation of her strength or lack thereof. Her knowledge, as it pertains to men, is demonically given to her. In other words, it's a form of sorcery. Ironically enough, one of the synonyms for the word "seductress" and "temptress" is "sorceress." A sorceress, as we all know, is a female witch. Believe it or not, the wiles and temptations of a seductress are pure witchcraft. The only difference between her and what most people think to be a witch is that she's not a hideous, warty woman stirring the contents of a big black pot, with a broom leaning on the rack nearby; nor is she a middle-aged, slightly overweight woman twirling her hands around a crystal ball. Her words are her powers and that's why you'll notice that whenever the Bible speaks of her, it speaks mostly of her words.

Proverbs 2:16 (ESV): So you will be delivered from the forbidden woman, from the adulteress with her smooth words.

Proverbs 22:14 (ESV): The mouth of forbidden women is a deep pit; he with whom the LORD is angry will fall into it.

Proverbs 30:20 (ESV): This is the way of an adulteress: she eats and wipes her mouth and says, "I have done no wrong."

Most seductresses don't know what they're doing wrong. It doesn't matter who they seduce or why they are seducing that person; they will find some way to justify their behaviors. Their justifications will not make sense to anyone who has a sound mind, but they will make sense to themselves.

Soul ties are powerful and Satan knows this. Ungodly soul ties create a bridge of sorts between the people who are bound by them. Your soul is comprised of your mind, will and emotions; therefore, when Satan seeks to create a soul tie with you, he is seeking to gain control of or your thinking ... or at least influence it. He is also seeking to control your feelings. The reason for this is that our thinking patterns and feelings are the driving forces behind our choices. If a man is saved and has the Holy Spirit, Satan will seek to enter that man's soul. In other words, the purpose of a soul tie is to give Satan access to the believer. Think of it this way. We are all temples; we are buildings. Let's say that a man got saved and was delivered from lust and every other sin that gave Satan access to him. Now, Satan is standing on the outside trying to find some way to get back in. He needs an invite to come in and he knows that the man in question wouldn't invite him in if he were to come as himself. He needs a mask and a costume and he needs the ability to disguise his voice to gain entry. He watches that man day after day to see what it is that he wants the most.

One day, while peering into the windows of that man's soul (we will call him William), Satan notices that he is fascinated with a dark-complexioned woman called Brenda, who attends the same church that he attends. Satan checks her out and discovers that she has not forgiven the last man who's hurt her;

therefore, she is accessible to Satan because of her unforgiveness. This is great news to the devil. He then realizes that he can use her as bait.

Brenda is a great woman who loves God and she plans to be a faithful wife to her husband someday. Satan decides to use her to fish William out of God's will, so Satan uses her unforgiveness to access her. He then causes her to have dreams of marrying William. At one point, she hadn't noticed the guy, but all of a sudden, she is interested in him because she believes that her dream came from God. Brenda does not test the spirit behind the dream, so she looks at William one Sunday morning and smiles at him. Her smile is an invitation to him and he accepts the invite. After church, he approaches the beautiful young woman of God and they exchange numbers. One year later, they are married and Satan now has access to William through his new wife.

Brenda is a good wife indeed, but her unforgiveness makes it impossible for her to fully give herself to her husband. Nevertheless, because she is now one with her husband, the enemy now has the bridge he needs to access that man's purpose, finances and peace.

One day, Satan notices that William is about to get promoted on his job; plus, God wants to bless him with a new car. Satan's not willing to let this happen, so he uses his bridge to hinder William. Before giving William this new promotion, his boss decides to test him. He asks him to work late for two weeks; after all, the new position will require that he work late hours some nights. When William tells Brenda that his boss wants him to work late, her unforgiveness flares up and she accuses him of having an affair. William tries to explain to his now pregnant wife that he is faithful and he tells her that he believes his boss is testing him to see if he is qualified for the promotion. Nevertheless, Brenda doesn't want to hear it.

She becomes even more argumentative and over the course of the next few days, she changes the atmosphere in the home. Now, the house feels cold, dark and very uncomfortable ... very much like a prison.

William accepts his boss's offer and works late, but he isn't very productive because not only is he distracted by what's going on at home, but Brenda keeps calling him and threatening to end their relationship. William's boss comes into the office and notices that William is distracted every night and doesn't get much work done, so he decides to give the promotion to Ben. Ben gets the promotion, the company car and his pay is doubled. Do you see how Satan used Brenda to hinder William? Believe it or not, this is very common. Satan is always trying to find a bridge that allows him to have access to a man and he will use anyone he can use, including an undelivered woman in the church.

When most people think of a seductress, they think of a sexually seductive woman who uses her feminine wiles to seduce men, but this is not always true. The most powerful seduction comes in the form of words. Notice that the word "seduce" is very much like the word "seed." It is also similar to the word "reduce". To seduce a man is to plant a seed in him that was designed to reduce him. One of the most effective seductions comes in the form of an emotional affair. In this, what happens is the woman uses whatever access she has to a man to gain his trust and sow seeds into his heart. This is why the Bible tells us to guard our hearts, for out of it pours the issues of life (see Proverbs 4:23). Understand that the heart is a garden and God's enemy is always looking to sow seeds in that garden.

Matthew 24:13-30 (ESV): He put another parable before them, saying, "The kingdom of heaven may be compared to a man who sowed good seed in his field, but while his men were sleeping, his enemy came and sowed weeds among the wheat and went away. So when the plants came up and bore grain, then the weeds appeared also. And the servants of the master of the house came and said to him, 'Master, did you not sow good seed in your field? How then does it have weeds?' He said to them, 'An enemy has done this.' So the servants said to him, 'Then do you want us to go and gather them?' But he said, 'No, lest in gathering the weeds you root up the wheat along with them. Let both grow together until the harvest, and at harvest time I will tell the reapers, "Gather the weeds first and bind them in bundles to be burned, but gather the wheat into my barn."'"

A great example of an effective emotional affair is a story that we hear all too often. A professional, married man hires a beautiful secretary. She is able to slither into his office and gain his wife's trust by claiming to have a boyfriend or a fiance. At first, all is well. She does a great job around the office and even seems to be supportive of that man's marriage.

One day, the man comes into the office and he opens up to his new secretary about his marriage. Just like any marriage, it's not perfect, so the new secretary begins to encourage the man and even give him some really good advice. She helps him to understand his wife and because of this, he begins to trust her more. Little does he know, the trap has been set and it's only a matter of time before Satan springs forward and ambushes him. Time after time, he turns to his secretary for personal issues and to get her professional opinion as well. He discovers that he can talk to her about things that he is uncomfortable talking to his wife about, and before long, he finds himself attracted to her. She doesn't "appear" to be attracted to him, but she is. She behaves like a friend and not-so-much like a woman who's flirting with a man. This is a part of her deception. Once Satan has ensnared the man and gotten him into her trap, he begins to lure him away from his wife. To do this, Satan will cause that man to compare his wife to his secretary. He will compare what he knows about his wife to what he believes about his secretary. His secretary appears to be sweet, understanding and easy to talk to, but his wife's attitude depends on his attitude. His secretary even keeps a Bible on her desk and quotes scriptures to him anytime he's feeling down. "God laid you on my heart last night," she says. "I sensed something was wrong, so I was up half the night praying for you and your wife." He smiles. The previous night he had been arguing with his wife. How does his secretary know that he was having problems at home? The answer is obvious. Her knowledge was demonically given to her. The scent of her seduction is luring him further and further away from God and his wife.

Satan then starts causing that man to magnify the issues that he has at home with his wife, all the while magnifying what he feels are the advantages of being with his secretary. One year later, he is divorcing his wife and planning to marry the weapon that was formed against him and his marriage. She's young, beautiful and brilliant; that's what he sees. But what he does not see is that she is naïve, ungodly (spiritually unattractive) and foolish. Three years into his marriage with his secretary, his company is on the brink of closing and his new wife's fangs have all but ripped him to shreds. He's come to realize that his new wife is still obsessed with her ex; plus, she doesn't know how to manage money, so she spends frivolously. Most of the money she spends is to impress her friends and to impress her ex. Nevertheless, she is beautiful to look at. What he doesn't realize is that her assignment was to destroy his marriage and swallow him whole ... and she's just about finished. Right now, she's just depleting him of his money. It is then that he looks back over his life and realizes that the most stable and peaceful time he had was when he was married to his first wife. It's too late, however, because the first wife has remarried and is now another man's favor.

This story is designed to serve as a warning to the men who Satan has put a hit out on. He doesn't send assassins wearing camouflage and carrying guns to assassinate you; his favorite (and most effective) weapon are beautiful (immoral) women wearing high heels and carrying Bibles. Believe it or not, these women are assassins.

The seductress is a powerful weapon formed against men simply because she doesn't look like, sound like or behave like a weapon. Her looks, her charm and her clothing are the lures she uses to draw men to her, but she ensnares them with her words. Consider Salome, the step daughter of Herod Antipas. She danced for her stepfather at his birthday party; this was the lure. But once Herod asked her what she wanted, she turned to her wicked mother, Herodias, and Herodias told her to ask for John the Baptist's head on a platter. This is very similar to what an adulteress does. She will seduce a man with her body and she will charm him with her words. She then gets him to a place where he feels the need to offer up something to her. Oftentimes, this happens before he lies with her. She then requests that he leave his wife and he agrees. Once the deed has been done, the man will oftentimes decide that he doesn't want to leave his wife. Nevertheless, his mistress continues to pursue him with her words, using sex as a bargaining tool. Eventually, in most cases, the man decides that he wants to stay with his wife and must leave his mistress alone. It is then that the adulteress will begin harassing his wife. Why is this? Because when the husband had sex with her, he let her in his life and gave her legal access to everything that's important to him (his marriage, his wife, his children, his name, his money, etc.). She will then use that access to finish off his marriage. She will not release that man until his marriage has been destroyed or he truly repents and gets delivered from her. If a man has slept with a seductress, he can't just walk away from her; he has to be delivered from her. Sure, he can physically walk away from her, but the soul tie he has with her will allow what is in her to have repeated access to him.

The seductress has the power to:
1. Change a man's thinking patterns.
2. Change the way a man sees his wife.
3. Destroy a man's marriage.
4. Destroy a man's name.
5. Cause a man to abandon his own children to raise the children she's birthed for other men.
6. Cause a man to turn his back on his own mother if she objects to his relationship with her.
7. Bring a man to financial ruin.
8. Cause a man to abandon his faith in God or cause him to rebel against God.
9. Convince a man that the seducer is his

favor (God-appointed wife).

10. Usher a man into the hands of Satan, all the while, convincing him that the seductress loves him.

It is of no wonder that the word "seductress" is synonymous with the word "sorceress." She's not a beautiful, helpless creature who's gonna make some man a great wife. In short, she is a devourer. How do I know? I was once her! I once had that devil in me; plus, my closest friends were temptresses. Because God delivered me from that devil and from the shame of my past, I can now warn others. A seductress, temptress, adulteress, mistress, enchantress or sorceress (whichever word you prefer) is the very opposite of favor; she is destruction in disguise.

Demonic Deployment

Spiritual warfare is very much like natural warfare. Satan doesn't just recruit soldiers; he links them up with other soldiers and then, deploys them. The reason for this is he needs to re-affirm the beliefs of every woman he has ushered (or snatched) into the darkness. When a woman is surrounded by people who think like her, she is less likely to abandon her ungodly belief system. The people around her validate her beliefs and can relate to her. Nevertheless, before Satan brings her together with her co-combatants, he must first help her to develop a set of ungodly beliefs.

Demonic friendships not only validate a woman's ungodly beliefs, but also help her to accept the reality that she's currently living in. When a woman sees that she is not the only one who's lived through hardships, her

confidence will begin to rise. This is a good
thing if her heart and mind is right with Christ,
but when she's still in darkness, she will only
develop confidence in the darkness. This
means it would be hard to win her to Christ.
Her friends will serve as tools to help Satan
keep her from leaving the darkness, just as he
will use her to keep her friends from escaping
him as well.

When I was a teenager, I remember having a
close friend who was near to my age (I think
she was twelve or thirteen and I was a year
older than her). We'll call her Evelyn. Evelyn's
mother had a live-in boyfriend who was very
controlling. He was always putting Evelyn and
her sister on punishment; plus, they'd gotten a
phone line for Evelyn's room, but he'd
demanded that they not give the number to
anyone. At first, we all just thought he was
being a very dominant, but harmless, step-
parent. Howbeit, as time went on, we were all
proven wrong. "Larry" had some even darker

demons than we'd initially thought.

One day, I heard a knock on my door and I went to answer it. It was a tearful Evelyn. She didn't want to come in the house (likely because my siblings were there), so she asked me to come outside.

Evelyn began to explain to me that Larry had made a sexual advance towards her. I could tell that she didn't know what to do. She was furious at Larry, but afraid to tell her mother. I believed that her mother was super-confident and would kick Larry out, so I insisted that she tell her. She finally agreed.

I don't remember if it was the same day or the next day, but I heard another knock on the door. It was Evelyn again. Again, she insisted that I come outside and I did. I noticed that Evelyn was holding the left side of her face. She removed her hand and I could clearly see a hand print on her face. She then went on to explain to me that she'd taken my advice and told her mother, but her mother hadn't responded how I thought she would. She accused Evelyn of lying about Larry and then, she proceeded to slap her. I could tell that her mother's response hurt her far more than what Larry had done. Eventually, the relationship between Larry and Evelyn's mother dissolved for other reasons, but Evelyn's relationship with her mother was never the same after that.

I noticed that most of the women I was surrounded with were like me. They had all been sexually abused and we could all relate to one another, but at different degrees. Of course, at that time, I didn't share everything because I was a teenager. I was super self-conscious and worried what my friends would think of me.

As I got older, I continued to meet new friends, most of whom were sexually immoral. They had all been molested, raped or fondled at some point in their lives. Like me, our experiences were not something we discussed, even though we'd testified to one another at some point about our pasts.

My friends and I were young, attractive women who loved to party and get the attention of men. Truthfully, we all just wanted to be loved and we paid varying prices in our attempts to acquire love. Most of us were relationship-oriented; meaning that our goal was to have long-term relationships that led to marriage. We weren't just randomly sleeping with men. A few others were opportunistic, wherein, they simply wanted whatever they could get from a man ... be it sex, money or compliments. We were an army of seductresses and this worked in our favor with men. We stormed clubs, danced seductively (a couple of them danced like guys) and emanated an enormous amount of confidence. We drew energy from one another. Amazingly enough, demons do the same thing; they draw strength from each other, and that's why you'll notice that deliverance ministers will oftentimes isolate them to cast them out.

My friends and I were an army and Satan had deployed us to entertain the men who were already in the darkness. This is very similar to what shrine prostitutes did. The men would go to the temple to worship Baal, Asherah, Tammuz or a host of other demons. They'd go through several experiences while there, including making sacrifices to their gods, eating some of the meat from their sacrifices, tasting wine, enjoying entertainment and so on. The final room was called the Venus room (at the temple of Baalbek); this is where the temple prostitutes were. Of course, the men could go in and have sex with any of the available men or women in that room.

What I learned is that in every level of demonic activity, Satan has set aside some women who are willing to indulge the men who are on their levels. If a man goes to the lowest pits in darkness, he will find women there who are willing to lustfully entertain him. If he goes to the high places in darkness, he will find women there who are willing to lustfully entertain him. Satan has women who will happily go into the prisons and have conjugal visits with unrepentant murderers, rapists and the like. He also has women who will walk into a church and go after every type of man in that church, from the parking lot attendants to the pastor of that church. He has discipled immoral women to do these dirty deeds and many of them travel in packs, while others, are lone-runners.

Each woman that Satan uses has been deployed to go after a certain type of man, and every time Satan decides to "promote" her, he simply allows her to gain the attention of men who are greater than the men she once settled for. A woman who once dated a prison-bound drug dealer may suddenly find herself on a date with an up and coming artist. This may not sound like very much of a promotion, but to her, it is. It will change the face (or faces) of the men she allows into her life. When Satan sees that he can trust her on the level that she's at, he will promote her once again, but this time, you may find her on a date with a man who owns a record company, and then, with a man who has already garnered success in the industry that Satan has assigned her to. Every promotion she gets is preceded by a broken heart and a new set of beliefs. She will meet new friends who are at the level she's being promoted to ... women who've mastered being broken. These women may look like friends and identify themselves as friends, but Satan has not sent them to entertain her; they are there to train her. Some will break her even more, but they will all validate her new beliefs.

Spiritual Whorefare

When an immoral woman asks for a man's number, what's in her is asking for permission to attack that man. Satan's most effective weapon is a devil wearing high heels and hiding behind a sultry voice. Satan's most effective weapon in the church is a Bible-toting, seductive woman who has more wiles than she has Word. She is a snare, or better yet, a death trap.

Ecclesiastes 7:26 (KJV): And I find more bitter than death the woman, whose heart is snares and nets, and her hands as bands: whoso pleaseth God shall escape from her; but the sinner shall be taken by her.

What is spiritual whorefare? The answer is obvious if put in an imaginative perspective: it's spiritual warfare, but the soldiers aren't iron-clad men riding horses and yielding swords.

They're wearing high heels and driving convertibles. It is also blind men who see women as mere objects.

I purchased a program called Rosetta Stone some years ago because I wanted to learn French. In the beginning, I participated in the program daily and I did learn a few French words. I was married to a French speaking man, so I wanted to be able to communicate with his family. Nevertheless, I gave up on the program after he revealed to me that not everyone speaks French the same. It's similar to English; some people have Southern accents (Georgia), some people have Eastern accents (New York), some have Western accents (California) and some have Cajun accents (Louisiana). There are varying accents in each region; for example, people from Kentucky have strong Southern accents, but they don't speak like people from Mississippi. Someone from the North may not notice the difference, but someone from the South will. Additionally,

people in England and people in South Africa
pronounce some English words differently than
the way we pronounce them in the States.
Some of the words, my ex said, were not
pronounced the way his family or most French-
speaking people would say them. Lastly, I
needed to be immersed in a language to
properly learn it; otherwise I'd learn a few
French words and statements, but that would
be it.

A relative of his was married to an American
woman and she went to his country to learn
their language. She immersed herself in the
language until she learned it. It was easier for
her to learn because she surrounded herself
with French-speakers. This is similar to what
Satan is doing in his war against men and
women.

A man is immersed in our sexually immoral
culture from the moment he wakes up until he
lays his head down at night. If he turns on the

morning news, he will more than likely see a scantily-clad woman on the television ... whether she's the news anchor or a woman who invades his eyes through a commercial. When he leaves and goes to work, he will more than likely come across one or more women wearing revealing clothing in the workplace. When he stops at the supermarket, he will see one or more scantily-clad women shopping alongside him. When he goes to church, he will see women wearing short mini-skirts sitting next to him. Everywhere he turns, his world will be invaded by the spirit of seduction. What's happening is Satan is teaching him how to speak the language of darkness. He immerses most American and Western men in sex-obsessed cultures so that they can speak the language of seduction. He does the same with women.

A woman is told how to look and behave from the moment she wakes up to the moment she lies down. Media is always depicting what it says is beautiful and contrasting it what we see as normal. She's basically told that she's not attractive as she is and that she needs to be "sexier." In other words, she's tempted to be tempting.

Satan is always putting up "wanted ads" for temptresses and these marketing schemes have been rather successful. This is to bait the women in. He then uses the women who take his bait and makes bait out of them. He shows them the lives that they want. It's similar to what he did with Jesus. Satan took Jesus up on a mountain and told Him that everything He saw would be His if He would fall down and worship him. Nevertheless, Jesus rebuked him and sent him away.

Satan takes women up to high places in their imaginations. That's why the Bible tells us to "cast down" imaginations and every "high thing" that exalts itself against the knowledge of God (see 2 Corinthians 10:5). Satan then uses

their voids, pain and desires to help him tailor-
make fantasies for each individual woman. He
then uses those fantasies as mental
commercials to draw them into his scheme.
When God told us to cast down imaginations,
He was telling us to cut them off; do not watch
the commercials. Whatever is not cast down
will eventually have to be cast out.

If the woman buys into Satan's lies, he then
begins to train her to be a soldier in his army.
He places her on the front lines of his war, but
is not truthful with her. He tells her that he's
teaching her to get the desires of her heart. In
her mind, she thinks that she's just "playing the
game" of life and weeding out the wrong men
to get to the right one. If he can convince her
to put on scanty clothing, which is the uniform
of an immoral woman, he will. If he cannot
convince her to wear this uniform, he will teach
her to use other methods to lure men to her.
Of course, she doesn't hear Satan talking
audibly to her; everything comes in the form of

imaginations and ideas. From there, the trap is set and the bait has been sent out to capture any man who is not guarded by holiness.

To capture men, Satan depicts several demonic personalities in movies and casts them as good women. For example, the Delilah spirit is often cast as beautiful, fun, seductive and understanding. Jezebel is often cast as a good woman who's been wounded. According to Satan's media, she just needs the love of a good man to help her to rise again. He also appeals to the man via the soulish realm through music and music videos. Delilah is often shown on music videos showing off her beautiful form. She appears fun, submissive and ready to please her man. Satan's goal is to get the man to want the woman, relate to his depiction of the woman and sympathize with her. In some cases, when he's introducing hatred to the man, he doesn't want him to relate to her. He wants him to hate her, but at the same time, he wants him to physically desire her.

Satan then invades the man's life with physical billboards, ads, commercials and live viewings of scantily clad women. He couples what he immerses the man in with that man's personal experiences in life to create a theory in his heart and mind. He ensures that most men are attracted to a "type," but in reality, they are attracted to certain types of demonic spirits. Like humans, demons have personalities, but unlike humans, their personalities are not individual to each devil. If you come across five hundred demons of lust, they will all have the same personalities, but they will manifest in different ways in different people. How they manifest depends on their assignments against that person, coupled with how much access they have to that person.

The man will pursue his "type", but he'll keep finding himself going through the same ordeal with different women. Of course, each incident will vary in degree of intensity and each incident will impact that man's belief system. Slowly, but surely, he will give Satan more access to his mind, will and emotions.

Think about fishing. Every type of fish in the lake, sea or ocean has certain fish types, amphibians, reptiles, and insects that they prefer to consume. Bass prefer to eat frogs, crayfish and lizards; whereas catfish prefer to eat aquatic plants, seeds and other small fish. Because of its size, an adult shark prefers its prey to be pretty sizable. It will eat larger fish, seals, sea lions and even attempt to eat humans. Sharks are opportunistic; meaning they'll eat whatever is made available to them at any given moment. This is similar to how men and women have "types".

Women who see themselves as nobodies will oftentimes go after men who lack ambition. Women who have high self-esteem or immeasurable confidence will oftentimes go after the bigger fish. They will reject any man who is not ambitious.

Men who see themselves as nobodies will oftentimes avoid settling down with women. They will be more like sharks, opportunistic lovers who will pretty much go for whatever woman is available to them at any given moment. At the same time, they won't settle with (or for) the women who dare to love them. Instead, they will take whatsoever they can get until the woman feels she has nothing left to give them.

Men who have high self-worth and are ambitious will oftentimes choose their women in accordance with their intentions. When they want sex, they will be opportunistic lovers, going after whichever women they have available to them at any given moment. When they want wife decoys (long-term girlfriends), they will go after women who they can present to their mothers, friends and colleagues. These women will oftentimes be ambitious, beautiful and sometimes, religious. Of course, their choice in women is oftentimes largely based on the people they want to impress the most, whether it be their mothers or their friends. When they want wives, they will oftentimes inquire about the character of the women in their sights. In many instances, these women will be mutually connected to someone they know. This isn't always the case as every man and woman is different, but it is standard practice. The gist of it is ... each man and woman will communicate with one another based on their intentions and their types.

Satan will continue to attack love (because God is love); plus he will continue to attack godly marriages by attacking the unmarried man and woman's view of marriage. He will encourage women to be more seductive and he'll do this by showing them people (in most cases, their own friends) who are engaged or married to men they've ensnared with their seductions.

Satan will make their engagements or marriages appear to be everything that each woman observing them wants. In this, he teaches the observer to be more immoral in her attempt to become a wife.

He will encourage men to entertain the lusts of their flesh by immersing them in this sex-obsessed culture. He does this to change their language and distort their views of women as a whole. This ensures that they will not desire to get married. Instead, they will constantly pour out their strength to immoral women.

Some fisherman use small bait (insects, small fish) to catch larger bait (small to medium-sized fish). They then use their catch to fish for even bigger fish. Satan works the same way. In this, Satan will bait the woman and then use her as bait to hook what he sees as a small man. In her relationship with this guy, she is actually being trained to hook an even bigger man.

When I was 18 or 19, I met a man who had a different type of spirit than the men I'd been dating. He was debonair and he wore his clothes properly. This was the man I spoke of earlier in this book (Wyatt). Wyatt changed my ideology; he changed my mind towards men. I thought I was just maturing, but in truth, Satan had given me a promotion. He'd broken, beaten, raped and abused me my whole life and, of course, this was to disciple me. He hadn't put all that work in to leave me in the hands of a petty rebel (that's how he sees them). Again, I didn't want a relationship with Wyatt because I didn't think I was his type; plus, I didn't want Wyatt anywhere near my heart. I believed that he had the potential to shatter every fiber of my self-esteem and confidence and I didn't want to put that type of power in his hands. I focused on the reality of Wyatt and not the potential of who he could be. I did this intentionally to keep myself from "falling for" him.

After Wyatt, I met a man who would become a short-term fiancé. "Jason" was very handsome, somewhat debonair and seemingly well-rounded. He was ten years my senior, but I didn't care. I was mesmerized by Jason's handsome face, well-chiseled body and manly ways; that's all. Nevertheless, after dating Jason for close to a year, I ended the relationship. The point is ... Satan will use one man to train a woman for the next one. He will change a woman's "type" by either promoting or demoting her. This is advancing in spiritual whorefare.

Every time a woman's heart is broken, Satan promotes her because a broken heart is an open one. If she doesn't turn to God and let Him repair and replenish her, she will be easily accessible to the enemy and Satan wants to use her all the more. He'll remind her of her childhood, the many rejections she's endured and he'll tell her that her heartbreak is the result of her being "too nice". What he's doing is trying to increase the darkness in her so that he can use her as bigger bait. The further into darkness a person goes, the more damage they'll do to anyone who opens their hearts or lives to them.

Every time a man's heart is broken, Satan will promote him because his broken heart will be like a sponge. He'll receive any information that helps him to feel better about what he's going through and how to avoid ever going through it again. If he doesn't turn to God, Satan will fill him up with lies and Satan will use that time to distort his view of women. The goal here is to keep him from finding his favor (his wife) and to be swallowed up by the immoral woman. This is spiritual whorefare; it's dirty and painful, but it often produces the results that Satan wants it to produce.

Fishing in the Sanctuary

I want you to imagine a fishing line hanging in the sanctuary. At the end of that line is a hook attached to the back of a beautiful woman. She is a loyal member of the church. She's very nice, very soft-spoken and very giving. Her name is Shelia.

The pastor of that church happens to be a young, single man who's been praying to God to send him his God-appointed wife. Because he's the pastor (plus, he's handsome), he's used to women hitting on him, but he's determined to get past them all and find his favor. We'll call him Tony.

Tony notices Shelia because she's beautiful, soft-spoken and very faithful in her attendance. At the same time, she's not like the other single women. She's not throwing herself at the pastor, nor does she appear to be desperate.

Shelia is an ambitious woman with one child from a previous marriage. She's almost finished getting her Master's degree in Speech Pathology and she plans to go back and get a Doctorate degree in Speech Language and Hearing Sciences. Shelia appears to be the perfect candidate, but inside of Shelia lurks the very dark and very familiar Jezebel spirit.

Jezebel has been after Pastor Tony ever since he was a little boy. He'd suffered abuse at the hands of his Jezebel-infested mother, and he was raised by his Jezebel-infested grandmother. Everywhere the pastor has gone in life, he's found himself linked to a Jezebel spirit; nevertheless, he gave his life to Christ after one of his best friends got saved and invited him to church with him. Pastor Tony escaped the abuse, manipulation and control of his family and moved out of the state. After several years of helping out at his local church, he was elevated to a pastor.

Pastor Tony has escaped the clutches of Jezebel, but that demon wants him back. It knows that he's not going to return to the controlling arms of his mother; plus, his grandmother has already passed away, so Jezebel needs to find another way to re-enter Tony's life. It chooses to do so through Shelia.

Jezebel knows that it cannot re-enter Tony's life the way it left; otherwise, he may recognize it, so it uses Shelia's soft-spoken voice and kind nature as a disguise. Satan has set the perfect trap for Tony and if he doesn't pray and clothe himself with the full armor of God, he will find himself unwittingly reconciling with Jezebel. If this happens, Jezebel will bring seven more demons who are more evil than she is. This is to ensure that Pastor Tony never gets free again.

Matthew 12:43-45 (KJV): When the unclean spirit is gone out of a man, he walketh through

dry places, seeking rest, and findeth none. Then
he saith, I will return into my house from
whence I came out; and when he is come, he
findeth it empty, swept, and garnished. Then
goeth he, and taketh with himself seven other
spirits more wicked than himself, and they
enter in and dwell there: and the last state of
that man is worse than the first. Even so shall it
be also unto this wicked generation.

Familiar spirits will oftentimes try to find their
way back to the people who've gotten free
from their evil grips, even if they have to come
into the sanctuary to do so. For this reason,
you will find many demonically influenced
women seated in churches, but not because
they want a Word from God. They are there
because they want Christian husbands. Most of
them don't know that the enemy is using them.
They simply know that they want to be loved
and they are attracted to men in church.

One story I often tell is of a female pastor who I

did business with some years ago. At that time, I was still somewhat young in the faith but I knew godly from ungodly. She'd hired me to design a logo for her ministry and while we were discussing her design needs, she suddenly struck up a conversation with me about men. I was married back then and I'd relayed that information to her, but somehow, that didn't seem to matter. She told me that she had a church and that she knew that nobody was going to go two years being sexually abstinent, so she told her members to simply get back up (after sex) and repent. She laughed as she told me that even she couldn't go two years without sex. As if this wasn't disturbing enough, she went on to tell me about a men's conference that was coming up. She said she would be going to that conference and I should too because there were going to be some "fine" men there. She was definitely a Delilah and she was fishing for leaders from the pulpit. Satan had disguised her as a leader to help her fish for other leaders. He needed "boots on the ground" in the church, but these boots had six inch heels and they were worn by an immoral woman posing as a prophetess.

My graphics business is tailored to ministries, so I've worked with thousands of ministries from around the world. Because of this, I can honestly say that I will not just walk into any random church. I've met some God-fearing, God-loving men and women of God, but I've also met some demonically influenced Devil Bait posing as leaders. They are unrepentant thieves and whoremongers who see ministry as a way to fatten their pockets and grow their influence. They range from angry Jezebels posing as "authoritative apostles" to self-seeking Delilahs posing as "submissive evangelists." They go into the sanctuary wearing all manners of dress, hoping to captivate the men with the greatest callings or followings. They've immersed themselves in church culture for so long that they can now speak, move and behave like true leaders, but their fruit will always fall from the tree and identify who they really are.

It goes without saying that many of their church's members are the same way. Often, I've observed many sexually immoral women who are incredibly beautiful (by today's beauty standards) go out of their way to get a seat at the front of the church. They want to be seen; they want to use whatever demonic powers the enemy has given them. They will sit at the front of a church and gaze seductively at the pastor or flash him an inviting smile. They are Devil Bait; they are the small fish who Satan is using to catch the big fish! Of course, some of these women are not after the pastor; they are after the men seated next to the pastor and the men in the congregation. When Satan identifies an anointing on a man, he will send demonically influenced women to captivate, or better yet, capture that man before he recognizes the call on his life. If he has already recognized the call on his life, Satan will try to capture him before he recognizes the size of the call on his life or before he starts walking in the office that he's called to. If he has started walking in his called place, Satan will send women to capture him so that he can use that man's influence and ruin his name. He also wants to capture that man before he finds his ticket to favor, better known as his wife.

Proverbs 22:1 (ESV): A good name is to be chosen rather than great riches, and favor is better than silver or gold.

Ecclesiastes 7:1 (ESV): A good name is better than precious ointment, and the day of death than the day of birth.

Proverbs 18:22 (ESV): He who finds a wife finds a good thing and obtains favor from the LORD.

I watched a video on YouTube where a man was interviewing a former witch. She was from Africa, but I don't remember what country she was from. Anyhow, she talked about how her desire to be rich and famous led her into witchcraft. It all started when a friend of hers told her that she could help her; this friend then took the woman to a river, began chanting, and then a demonic entity called "a mermaid spirit" emerged from the water. These types of stories are "amazing" to most Western believers, but they are common in many African countries where witchcraft is prevalent.

The woman said that she made her request known to the mermaid spirit and she entered into a covenant with that spirit. She was then assigned to sleep with a certain number of men on a daily basis. After a while, she was assigned to go after pastors. This story would have sounded incredible to me if much of what she'd said had not matched what God told me. One of the things she talked about was being able to tell which pastors were walking in holiness versus the ones who were not. She could easily seduce the ones whose lights were dim, but the ones who walked in holiness were surrounded by fire.

When I was in the world, I didn't go after religious leaders because I'd been brought up in and out of the church. I had a true fear of God and I knew not to touch a man of God. Nevertheless, when sizing men up for a potential relationship, I didn't know whether they were saved or not. I didn't know anything about holiness, but what I did know was that some men were off-limits. I didn't know why they were off limits, but anytime I came in contact with Christian men, I showed them the utmost respect. My friends were the same way. God places protection around His sons and daughters who walk in holiness, but a man or woman led astray by lust will be swallowed by Satan if they do not repent.

1 Peter 5:8 (ESV): Be sober-minded; be watchful. Your adversary the devil prowls around like a roaring lion, seeking someone to devour.

The above passage indicates that Satan cannot devour everyone. He goes about looking for someone he can devour. Undoubtedly, any man or woman not clothed with the armor of God will be on his menu. Additionally, the Bible talks about two types of minds when dealing with the seductress. In the above passage, the Bible says to be "sober-minded." What does this mean? It means to have a sound mind. God is saying to not be under the influence of lies. To have any other doctrine or message in you other than the true and uncompromising Word of God is to be bewitched, intoxicated and not operating from a sober mind. That's why Paul rebuked the Church of Galatia when they were dabbling in other doctrines. In Galatians 3:1, He said, "O foolish Galatians, who hath bewitched you, that ye should not obey the truth?"

Men who are not guarded by a sober-mind will be easily led astray or backslide when Satan dangles bait in front of them, whether they are at home or seated in the sanctuary.

Another mindset reference is a simple mind; meaning that the person in question is not guarded by wisdom, knowledge or understanding. This mindset is oftentimes attributed to young people.

Proverbs 7:4-9 (ESV): Say to wisdom, "You are my sister," and call insight your intimate friend, to keep you from the forbidden woman, from the adulteress with her smooth words. For at the window of my house I have looked out through my lattice, and I have seen among the simple, I have perceived among the youths, a young man lacking sense, passing along the street near her corner, taking the road to her house in the twilight, in the evening, at the time of night and darkness.

We need to understand that Satan does come to the body of Christ (church in general) to fish for men (and women) whom he can devour, but first, he has to bait his prey, draw them out of the will of God; then he will begin to swallow them whole.

The Devils Behind the Scenes

There are spiritual forces at work behind the
scenes of an immoral woman and these forces
want to remain hidden. The woman is just the
disguise they use to enter into the lives of the
people they want to attack. She is nothing but
a mask for them; she is nothing but bait to
them. She is driven by her voids, her lack of
understanding and her desire to repair the
damage done to her life (or ego) and she thinks
that she can do this with the help of a decent
man.

To capture her, demons had to first convince
her that her life would be much easier if she
had a man, and not just any man. She needed
to go after a certain type of men. Demons
oftentimes assign women to attack certain
classes of men and or men with a specific
anointing. This is why most women have a

"type". Unbeknownst to each individual woman, her type is nothing but the type or types of demons she's used to romantically engaging herself with. The reality is ... there are different types of demonic spirits and each one has its own function and carries its own unique assignment. For example, an unsaved or unchanged man who has an apostolic anointing (and is unaware of it) may find himself in one failed relationship after the other. Because of his strength, Satan would likely assign a few Delilahs to him, hoping to get him to impart something very valuable into each woman: his strength (authority) and his seed (children). Understand this: a godly woman is clothed with strength; she is a fountain of blessings, but an immoral woman is the door to a bottomless pit. She is an open grave where blind men go to die.

Proverbs 31:3 (ESV): Do not give your strength to women, your ways to those who destroy kings.

Proverbs 23:27-28 (KJV): For a whore is a

deep ditch; and a strange woman is a narrow pit. She also lieth in wait as for a prey, and increaseth the transgressors among men. **Proverbs 31:23-25 (ESV):** Her husband is known in the gates when he sits among the elders of the land. She makes linen garments and sells them; she delivers sashes to the merchant. Strength and dignity are her clothing, and she laughs at the time to come.

When a man has sex with a woman, he becomes one with her. He imparts a part of himself into her. By doing so, he gives her access to the very essence of who he is, what he has and what he is called (or sent) to do. **1 Corinthians 6:15-16 (KJV):** Know ye not that your bodies are the members of Christ? Shall I then take the members of Christ, and make them the members of an harlot? God forbid. What? Know ye not that he which is joined to an harlot is one body? For two, saith he, shall be one flesh.

Ever since I got involved in deliverance ministry, I've come to better understand not only how demons get in, but how they work. We all have a purpose; we have an assignment in Christ Jesus and the enemy does not want anyone to carry out their assignments. Why? Because he hates us and because he's jealous of our relationship with God. He knows that God wants to bless His people. God wants us to live healthy, happy, abundant lives filled with joy and laughter. God wants us to experience Heaven on Earth. Satan wants us to have the opposite of what God wants us to have. He wants to be our god; he wants us to worship him and he wants us to spend eternity in the lake of fire with him.

God has blessed me to conduct mass deliverance sessions on my prayer line and most of the people who come on the line are women. One of the most common spirits that manifests and is cast out during those calls is the spirit of rejection. This is one of Satan's most effective demons. Many women have been rejected by their natural fathers, rejected by their mothers and rejected by their peers. Sadly enough, many of them came into the church and were rejected by the members and the leaders. The way the spirit of rejection works is by teaching the person who's bound by it to be "different" but not in a good way. They stand out, even though they want to fit in. This is because the spirit of rejection will torment them and make them uncomfortable around people. They are afraid to be themselves with others because they have been rejected by some of the most influential people in their lives (parents, family members, peers) when they were simply being themselves. So, they are oftentimes talkative, controlling, prideful, seductive or overly careful. For example, one of my issues was being overly careful around the husbands of other women. I didn't want to send out the wrong signals or make the wives feel uncomfortable, so I'd speak mostly to the wives. This ended up having an adverse reaction; I would unintentionally make the wives uncomfortable because they noticed my discomfort around their husbands. Again, this is very common with people who have suffered rejection and the fear of rejection.

Another spirit that often manifests is called a spirit husband. In America, we often refer to this spirit as incubus. He is responsible for almost any and everything dealing with sexual immorality. Nevertheless, the spirit-husband's main entrance into a person's life is through witchcraft or through that person dabbling with the occult. For example, when a woman reads her horoscope, practices Yoga or has her palm read, she opens the door for a spirit husband. At the same time, the majority of the women who have this spirit didn't get it through sins of their own; it was a generational curse passed down to them by one or both of their undelivered parents. It was likely something that was passed down to their parents from their grandparents and from their great-grandparents to their grandparents. It will go undetected generation after generation until someone confronts it. Lastly, it can also enter in through sexual contact with others who are themselves bound.

When a spirit husband is in a woman, it will provoke lust in her. Ironically enough, it is a very wicked and jealous spirit, so it will not allow her to have long-term relationships. If she gets married, it will take away her sexual desire towards her husband. It will even cause her to despise him and become argumentative towards him. It will use her to tear down her marriage with her own hands. At the same time, if she is not married, it will attempt to drive away any man who gets too serious about her. It doesn't mind her being promiscuous because her promiscuity gives it access to every man she's slept with, but it is passionately against her being in any committed relationships.

When a woman is bound by the spirit husband, she may have trouble getting pregnant and will likely have issues in her reproductive organs (cysts, fibroid, Endometriosis, etc.).

On my prayer line, I had a girl who had been diagnosed with Endometriosis. She had tried everything and was ready to give up. The Lord told me that the culprit was a spirit husband, and He blessed me to take her through deliverance. Sure enough, the spirit husband manifested and when I began to divorce her from it, it started crying. This is what happens in many of the cases when a woman is delivered from a spirit husband; it will begin to cry and sometimes, even beg to keep what it believes to be its wife. Nevertheless, it is a wicked spirit; meaning that its intentions are wicked. That's why she had Endometriosis. It was tormenting her and trying to keep her to itself.

When a single woman is bound by a spirit

husband, she may love sex, but once she's married, her desire to have sex will likely fade away. The only exception to this rule is if the man she's married to has a call to ministry on his life, but has been bound by the enemy with the spirit of lust. In such cases, the enemy will use her to grow the lust in the man she's married to. In such a case, she will be sexually adventurous and open to all forms of perversion. What she doesn't know is that the man, in Satan's eyes, is a fish that he's fattening-up to bring down. Once he uses her to help that man to increase in perversion, he will use an even bigger bait (seductress) to fish him out of that marriage. Again, the spirit husband doesn't mind her being promiscuous because her sexual adventures allow him to capture more men, but when she enters a monogamous relationship, the spirit husband will do whatever it can to drive away, harm or even kill the man in her life.

A deliverance minister doesn't always have to

call out the names or the functions of the
demons to get them to respond or come out of
the people they are tormenting. Some spirits
respond once the deliverance minister calls out
the door they entered in through. For example,
on my prayer line, anytime I call out demons
who entered in through sex, rape or
molestation, there is oftentimes a large
response. Of course, there are many demons
that can enter into a person through sex, since
sex creates a soul-tie and that soul tie serves
as a bridge between both parties. Additionally,
every demon that enters in through sex isn't
necessarily a "sex spirit" or a spirit of lust.
Sometimes, the spirits that enter are double-
mindedness (schizophrenia), poverty, infirmity,
premature death, obsession, etc. This is just a
small list of the demons that can build a bridge
between two souls and cross over between
those souls to wreak havoc. Demons love
ungodly soul-ties because they grant them
access to more souls. They don't just transfer
from one person to the next (they will never

leave one person to be with another); instead, they simply build a bridge and attack both souls. Demons are territorial and see people as property. They are always trying to increase their territory.

When a woman is raped, molested or sexually assaulted in any way, the attack is more spiritual than it is physical. The person attacking her is demonically possessed, and for that person, the attack is more about power than it is about sexual gratification. Sure, the person may be aroused sexually, but most rapists have access to people who are willing to have sex with them (girlfriends, wives, etc.). The reality is ... sex isn't just about sexual gratification; it's centered around the entire experience. It's centered around overpowering another person, terrorizing another person (demons love fear), controlling another person through fear (demons love to feel like gods) and the adrenaline rush that the attack brings to the attacker. All of these things come together and intensify the experience for the rapist. Many convicted rapists, including serial rapists, were married men. Again, it wasn't just about the sex for them; it was about power.

When a man physically restrains a woman, he is using his power to override hers. In other words, what is in him is trying to take dominion over her.

Ephesians 6:12 (NIV): For our struggle is not against flesh and blood, but against the rulers, against the authorities, against the powers of this dark world and against the spiritual forces of evil in the heavenly realms.

Demons like power; they like to control others. They want to be our god. As a matter of fact, Satan was jealous of God and this is what led to the events that got him kicked out of Heaven. Since it is difficult for demons to wholly possess an individual, they try to garner as much power as possible over each person that they have access to. They get access to people through generational curses, sins, ungodly media, friendly associations, romantic relationships, occult associations (palm reading, horoscopes, Ouija boards) and the list goes on. When they gain access to an individual, they cannot override that person's will, so they will slowly teach that person to come into agreement with them. They do this by bringing a series of events upon that person and then using their access to that person's soul (mind, will and emotions) to offer remedies for whatever opposition that person is faced with. This is called suggestive brainwashing. Let's say for example's sake that the person in question is a woman who was raped by her ex-boyfriend. Slowly, but surely, the demons in her will change her thinking patterns by making her relive her rape. They will tell her that her ex is enjoying his life while she is being tormented. They will cause her to become obsessed with him, but this obsession won't be romantic in nature; it will be an obsession with getting revenge. Let's call this woman Mona and her rapist Jerry.

Mona tries to move on with her life and she learns to function in her dysfunction. Mona gets married to a wonderful man named Stephen, but because of what she's gone through, Mona finds it hard to fully enjoy sex with her husband. Their dark bedroom makes it even scarier, so Mona must sleep with the lights on. Mona tries to be a good wife, but she's emotionally unavailable. She busies herself by working two jobs and being constantly animated, so Stephen begins to feel abandoned in his own marriage. Eventually, Mona and Stephen's marriage ends and Mona loses one of her jobs. She tries to find another job to replace the one that she's lost, but no one calls her back. When she gets off from her first job, Mona is finally home by herself and left alone with her own thoughts. She doesn't think about the rape, nor does she think about her rapist, but she's tormented by feelings of worthiness, depression, and suicidal thoughts. She is reminded that everyone who comes in contact with her either hurts or abandons her. Many questions plague her mind. Why did Stephen leave her? Why didn't he think she was good enough for him? Satan will place those types of questions in a woman's mind, and then he will proceed to answer them. In her mind, she begins to reason that men are evil creatures who are selfish, perverted and insensitive. Once she believes this, she will accept it as truth. Anytime we receive something as true, it becomes a part of our belief system and begins to navigate our choices by changing our thinking patterns. This is how demons get behind the "will" of our lives and begin to brainwash us. If they can change your beliefs, they can change the course of your life.

Mona decides that she is going to be to men what they were to her: emotionally unavailable. She will get what she wants from them and abandon them the very minute they begin to do anything similar to what Jerry or Stephen did.

Do you see how the enemy has now gotten behind the "will" of Mona's life? They will then send more men into her life to further damage her. She will find herself on the arms of broken men, men who Satan will use to break her even more and men that Satan will use her to break. Before long, Mona's body (to her) is nothing more than a tool that she uses to get what she wants from men. Again, this is satanic discipleship. This is how a seductress is made.

In Mona's case, the spirits she will likely wrestle with include, but are not limited to:

- Rejection
- Bitterness
- Anger - Rage
- Vengeance
- Spite (a desire to hurt, annoy, offend)
- Unforgiveness
- Confusion
- Lust or hatred of sex
- Obsession

- Fear
- Fear of rejection
- Torment
- Memory recall

Believe it or not, these are all demonic spirits and I've witnessed the manifestation of every last one of these spirits. Mona will see the surface of the issue, but she won't see the spirit of it all. Every tree has a root and Satan loves to plant seeds in believers so that more ungodly trees will grow and flourish. We get caught up in blaming others for what they've done to us while the devils who've used them walk by unscathed.

Cultures and Concubines

There are biblical customs regarding marriage that most people in the church are unaware of. Because of this, the modern church has redefined the words fornication, marriage and whore. Over the years, our church culture has seen numerous changes and many aren't willing to address those changes. The reason for this is the agents of change have oftentimes been men and women who the church has come to respect. Truthfully, it's more than just respect; it has grown into full-blown reverence. Because of this, when a man (or woman) of God commits sexual immorality and is unrepentant, the divide in the church is made evident. One side of the church says that the leader is human and therefore, prone to mistakes (which, of course, is true). The other side says that the leader needs to understand his (or her) position; after all, he (or she) is influencing so many others (which, of course, is also true). Because of this reverence, many leaders are not corrected by those who are charged to hold them accountable. *This is especially true if the leader has a huge following.* Instead, they are taught to stiffen their necks and ignore the angry rants of the people who once trusted them to cover their souls. They are taught to label the people as "church people" and to keep on sinning, but from now on, they tell themselves that they need to be more discreet about their sins. We don't talk about these things, but this is truly what's happening in many of our sanctuaries. Satan's attack against the church has been very successful and adultery is quickly becoming a part of church culture.

Society (and the church) has altered several words to help our generation and the generations to come to continue wearing the badges of morality. When we see a particular sin becoming the norm, we must understand that we are witnessing a principality at work. At the same time, we are witnessing something that we, the church, have failed to come together and bind.

Matthew 18:18-20 (ESV): Truly, I say to you, whatever you bind on earth shall be bound in heaven, and whatever you loose on earth shall be loosed in heaven. Again I say to you, if two of you agree on earth about anything they ask, it will be done for them by my Father in heaven. For where two or three are gathered in my name, there am I among them."

Hebrews 10:25 (KJV): Not forsaking the assembling of ourselves together, as the manner of some is; but exhorting one another: and so much the more, as ye see the day approaching.

Instead, the common response to almost every ungodly change that has taken place has been to alter the words that we use to differentiate good from evil. By changing the words, we allow certain behaviors to become the norm, and unbeknownst to many, we also allow demonic spirits to be released against our nation and our church.

Isaiah 5:20 (ESV): Woe to those who call evil good and good evil, who put darkness for light and light for darkness, who put bitter for sweet and sweet for bitter!

Fornication: The word "fornication" comes from the Greek word "porneia" and it means "sexual immorality." It isn't just limited to sex outside of a godly marriage; sexual immorality covers what we have learned to call premarital sex, sodomy, masturbation, homosexuality, bestiality, etc. It is also defined as "idolatry." Of course, this is because a person who submits his or her body to sexual immorality is truthfully offering himself or herself up as a living sacrifice in exchange for whatever it is that they are hoping to get. Understand this: all sex is a trade-off; both people want something from the other person, even if what they want is love, marriage, peace or pleasure. Of course, the word "porneia" is where we get the word "porn" which is short for "pornography."

Marriage: There are customs centering around marriage that many in the church are not aware of. In the biblical days, Hebrews did not have weddings. What made a husband become a husband and a wife become a wife was SEX! Traditionally, a woman would be betrothed to a man. In many cases, it was her father who made an arrangement with the father of the man she was betrothed to marry. The men had what is the equivalent of a contractual agreement stating that their children would get married someday. Additionally, if the marriage was not arranged by the fathers, it would be the groom himself who arranged his marriage. The groom would ask the bride's father for his daughter's hand in marriage. If he agreed, the groom would pay a dowry. This dowry would be in the form of land, money, animals or services rendered. This secured the agreement. This arrangement was considered the equivalent of marriage.

When the day arrived for the marriage ritual, the groom would come to the house of his soon-to-be father-in-law. This was going to be what we call his "wedding day." The wife-to-be would wait with her maidens for the groom to arrive. Once he arrived, his father-in-law would hand him a white cloth, referred to as a "proof of virginity" cloth. He would then take his "fiancé" into a room called a "chuppah room". While the couple were in the chuppah room consummating their marriage, everyone else would be waiting and celebrating the marriage outside the room. Once the consummation was over, the groom would give the proof of virginity cloth to the bride's father or the witnesses chosen by the bride's father. This cloth would then be kept by the father or the bride to ensure that the groom could not bring any allegations of adultery against his new bride. (It was considered adultery for a betrothed woman to romantically entertain another man.) After the consummation, the bride, groom and their loved ones would head over to the groom's house to celebrate. It would be hundreds of years after the death of Christ Jesus before our traditional marriage ceremonies would be introduced.

What does this all mean? It's simple. Marriage isn't established at the alter; it's established in the bedroom, the backseat of a car, the living room floor or wherever sex takes place. What made it illegal was when there was no agreement between the father of the bride and the father of the groom-to-be or the father of the bride and the groom himself. Let's revisit the story of Jacob.

Genesis 29:1-30 (ESV): Then Jacob went on his journey and came to the land of the people of the east. As he looked, he saw a well in the field, and behold, three flocks of sheep lying beside it, for out of that well the flocks were watered. The stone on the well's mouth was large, and when all the flocks were gathered there, the shepherds would roll the stone from the mouth of the well and water the sheep, and put the stone back in its place over the mouth of the well.

Jacob said to them, "My brothers, where do you come from?" They said, "We are from Haran." He said to them, "Do you know Laban the son of Nahor?" They said, "We know him." He said to them, "Is it well with him?" They said, "It is well; and see, Rachel his daughter is coming with the sheep!" He said, "Behold, it is still high day; it is not time for the livestock to be gathered together. Water the sheep and go, pasture them." But they said, "We cannot until all the flocks are gathered together and the stone is rolled from the mouth of the well; then we water the sheep."

While he was still speaking with them, Rachel came with her father's sheep, for she was a shepherdess. Now as soon as Jacob saw Rachel the daughter of Laban his mother's brother, and the sheep of Laban his mother's brother, Jacob came near and rolled the stone from the well's mouth and watered the flock of Laban his mother's brother. Then Jacob kissed Rachel and wept aloud. And Jacob told Rachel that he was her father's kinsman, and that he was Rebekah's son, and she ran and told her father.

As soon as Laban heard the news about Jacob, his sister's son, he ran to meet him and embraced him and kissed him and brought him to his house. Jacob told Laban all these things, and Laban said to him, "Surely you are my bone and my flesh!" And he stayed with him a month.

Then Laban said to Jacob, "Because you are my kinsman, should you therefore serve me for nothing? Tell me, what shall your wages be?" Now Laban had two daughters. The name of the older was Leah, and the name of the younger was Rachel. Leah's eyes were weak, but Rachel was beautiful in form and appearance. Jacob loved Rachel. And he said, "I will serve you seven years for your younger daughter Rachel." Laban said, "It is better that I give her to you than that I should give her to any other man; stay with me." So Jacob served seven years for Rachel, and they seemed to him but a few days because of the love he had for her.

Then Jacob said to Laban, "Give me my wife that I may go in to her, for my time is completed." So Laban gathered together all the people of the place and made a feast. But in the evening he took his daughter Leah and brought her to Jacob, and he went in to her. (Laban gave his female servant Zilpah to his daughter Leah to be her servant.) And in the morning, behold, it was Leah! And Jacob said to Laban, "What is this you have done to me? Did I not serve with you for Rachel? Why then have you deceived me?" Laban said, "It is not so done in our country, to give the younger before the firstborn. Complete the week of this one, and we will give you the other also in return for serving me another seven years." Jacob did so, and completed her week. Then Laban gave him his daughter Rachel to be his wife. (Laban gave his female servant Bilhah to his daughter Rachel to be her servant.) So Jacob went in to Rachel also, and he loved Rachel more than Leah, and served Laban for another seven years.

Did you notice that there was no wedding in this story? Jacob likely got drunk at the feast and woke up next to Leah. He'd already had sex with her and that made her his legal wife. Of course, he was upset because he obviously wasn't attracted to Leah; he wanted Rachel. Nevertheless, Laban requested that he serve him another seven years to get Rachel's hand, and he did.

Did you also notice that he did not send Leah away? Jacob continued on with Leah because he could not legally put her away unless he could prove that she was not a virgin when he met her. Jacob went on to have seven children with Leah. They had six sons: Reuben, Simeon, Levi, Judah, Issachar, Zebulun; and one daughter: Dinah.

This means that we have a skewed understanding of what fornication is. Because of this, there are many married people walking around who have never had a formal wedding and many of them don't even know that they're married in God's eyes. Of course, we can repent and God can set us free; nevertheless, to repent, we must first understand what we are repenting for. There are many people who get married while soul tied (informally married) to other people and this is one of the reasons that divorce is so high, even in the church. When I got married formally the first time, I didn't know that I was already informally married! The only difference was ... my formal husband and I exchanged vows in the presence of two or three witnesses, but my informal husbands (past lovers) and I didn't have a formal agreement or any witnesses in place. This is what made our marriages illegal.

When God says "the two shall be one," He is talking about any two people who have sex with each other. This includes a man sleeping with a prostitute.

1 Corinthians 6:15-16 (ESV): Do you not know that your bodies are members of Christ? Shall I then take the members of Christ and make them members of a prostitute? Never! Or do you not know that he who is joined to a prostitute becomes one body with her? For, as it is written, "The two will become one flesh."

I teach a lot of women about waiting for their God-appointed husbands and many have been asking God to send them their husbands for years. God had me to tell many of them that they couldn't receive the husbands they'd been praying for because they were already married! They needed to approach the alter of God to be delivered from every illegal union that they'd entered; plus, they needed to be delivered from every demonic spirit that entered into their lives because of those unuions. This is also one of the reasons I ignore people who say to me that I could never remarry because the Bible says so. I understand that they are speaking from their cultural understanding of what marriage is and their misinterpretation of the scriptures. Many of them are women who are lying next to their formal husbands, not even realizing that they have several informal husbands. They've made themselves the concubines of many men, but because of today's church culture, they are ignorant of their own conditions. They are what Jesus described as people who have a plank in their eyes, but are distracted by the planks in other folks' eyes.

Matthew 7:5 (NIV): You hypocrite, first take the plank out of your own eye, and then you will see clearly to remove the speck from your brother's eye.

Additionally, the Bible does tell us when divorce is permitted and in both cases, my divorces were legally permitted by God because in both cases, I was married to unbelievers who committed adultery and left.

1 Corinthians 7:15 (ESV): But if the unbelieving partner separates, let it be so. In such cases the brother or sister is not enslaved. God has called you to peace.

Matthew 5:31-32 (ESV): "It was also said, 'Whoever divorces his wife, let him give her a certificate of divorce.' But I say to you that everyone who divorces his wife, except on the ground of sexual immorality, makes her commit adultery, and whoever marries a divorced woman commits adultery.

Whore: I remember being a new babe in Christ and sitting in the sanctuary on a Sunday morning. My pastor was teaching on the term "whoremonger" and he had my full attention. He said something that I didn't know but which my spirit bore witness to. He told us the biblical definition of the word "whoremonger." A whore, biblically speaking, isn't just a woman who's slept with multiple men; a whore is any woman who's had sex with a man who wasn't formally her husband. That truth hit me hard. I was a whoremonger and I couldn't deny it anymore. I was sexually immoral and I could not claim to be a Proverbs 31:10-31 woman. As time went on, I studied the word "whore" and got a better definition of it.

The word "whore" comes from the Hebrew word for prostitute: "qadesh." Qadesh is the masculine word for "prostitute." Again, in our culture, because promiscuity is common, we've changed the word "whore" to mean a sexually promiscuous woman. In my generation, a woman wasn't considered promiscuous unless she'd slept with multiple men at one time or within a short period of time. The word "girlfriend" protected her from wearing the "whore" tag. This is the reason that I didn't realize that I was a whore. At the same time, when I got a better understanding of the word "prostitute," I had to acknowledge that I was a prostitute. The only difference between me and a woman who exchanged sex for money is that I exchanged sex for love; plus, my lovers had to spend countless months, days and hours with me. For me to have sex with them, they had to convince me that they loved me, introduce me to their loved ones and make me think that we had a future together as husband and wife. Those were my terms. Did this make me any better than the street walker we've come to know as a "hooker"? No. I was deceived; I thought I was a good girl. They are honest about who they are and what they want.

Now, I'm not putting these terms out there to bash women. Truthfully, I believe that had we kept the original definitions of the words and not tried to re-brand Christianity, sexual immorality wouldn't be as common as it is today. We simply have a nation of deceived men and women and that's why God told us to study and show ourselves approved (see 2 Timothy 2:15).

Today, many people have a vicarious

relationship with God through their pastors;
meaning that they do not have a one-on-one
intimate relationship with the Lord. This also
means that they have to accept whatever is
fed to them. The good news is that there are
many God-fearing men and women of God out
who will not compromise the Word of God. The
bad news is that there are many men and
women who impersonate true leaders and they
are poisoning God's people with demonic
doctrines. This, of course, is the fault of the
people who eat from their tables. How so?
They do not have an intimate relationship with
God. Because they don't have a personal
relationship with God, they do not know His
voice, and therefore, they will follow the voice
of a stranger. This is how many demonic
cultures start in the church.

Another term we need to revisit is the word
"concubine." A concubine was a female slave
who also functioned as a secondary wife.
Many men in the Bible (especially powerful and

wealthy men) had concubines. Concubines were oftentimes sold by their fathers because their families were very poor. Nevertheless, the man who paid for a concubine was considered her husband and he referred to his father-in-law as his father-in-law. The concubine was a little lower than the wife, but she would be considered a great contender with the wife if she bore male children for her husband.

Men would also take concubines if their wives were barren or if their wives kept birthing female children. It was commonly believed at that time that women unconsciously determined the gender of their children. Women who bore male children, especially as their firstborns, were considered blessed. When Sarah sent Abraham to have sex with her maiden, Hagar, she was under the impression that she was too old and could not bear children. Once she gave birth to Isaac, she felt threatened by Hagar and her son because Hagar was the mother of Abraham's firstborn. Traditionally, the firstborn would receive the greatest blessing and during that time, the firstborn would oftentimes be with a woman considered to be a wife. The blessing went to the son of the woman who was officially considered a wife. This is why choosing which son to bless might have been difficult for Abraham. This is also likely why Sarah said that Ishmael (Hagar's son) would not be equal with her son, Isaac. Sarah likely feared that Isaac would lose his blessing to Ishmael or have to share it with him. As cruel as her petition seems, she was likely protecting her son. It was not uncommon for men to kill their own brothers to receive their inheritances and Sarah likely worried that this could be the fate of her son, especially when she witnessed Ishmael mocking him.

Again, a man had wives and he had concubines. The wives had come from normal or wealthy families, whereas the concubines had come from poor families. The concubines were slaves, oftentimes assigned to help the women who were considered to be wives.

The point is ... concubinage isn't dead. It is still very much practiced today. The only difference between now and then is that the men took their concubines in as wives. They provided for them and their children. We can't speculate that the "main wives" were okay with their husbands sleeping with other women. It was simply culture and it wasn't a sin because there was no law that disallowed this.

Today, there are many men who have "main wives" and they have mistresses which, of course, are nothing but illegal concubines. Some men (and women) would reason that this practice is and was acceptable by God, but this is not true. There was simply no rule against this; therefore, it wasn't necessarily a sin. Concubinage amongst the Messianic Jews was done away with after the death (and resurrection) of Jesus Christ.

Today's concubines are not like the ones David, Solomon and Abraham had. How is this? To be qualified to be a concubine in the biblical days, the woman had to either be a virgin, a widow or a victim of rape who'd been declared innocent. Today, most of the women who play the mistress are illegally married to several men. They are demonically assigned to destroy marriages. In exchange for their "services," Satan pretty much promises to give them the desires of their hearts. That desire, in most cases, is another woman's husband. What's amazing about the mistress is that after her assignment is complete and she's aided the husband in destroying his marriage, she will likely lose interest in him. Again, I was surrounded by immoral women and this was the norm. They didn't know why they'd lost interest in the men they were seeing. What they didn't realize was that they'd entered a race and in that race, they were competing against the wives of their suitors. When they ran that race, they thought that the reward they wanted was the man himself, but anytime they won a race, they discovered that the real reward for them was winning. It was simply a competition that the mistress wanted to win. She wanted to see if she looked better, cooked better and was better in the bedroom than her suitor's wife. In layman's terms, she wasn't pursuing the man; she was on the heels of that man's wife. Winning made her feel better about herself or it validated a belief that she had. Truthfully, in most cases, the other woman's presence in that marriage was her response to having been abandoned by another man. Most guys don't know this, but all too often, women go after the husbands of other women because some guy left them to be with someone else. *This is how they redeem their own self-worth.* They entered one contest and lost, so they enter a new one, but this time, they give themselves the upper-hand. How so? They have come to realize that a married man is familiar with his wife, but new relationships are oftentimes exciting because both parties don't truly know one another. This allows them to "fill in the blanks" to whichever questions they have about one another. Both people will oftentimes fall in love with their perceptions of who the other person is, what that person represents and what he or she can bring into their lives. This is nothing short of a bewitching.

When I lived in darkness, I found myself being in the midst of many women who were immoral in different ways and I remember being fascinated with them all. *I think we were all fascinated with one another's tactics.* I was amazed at how different each woman reasoned or justified her behaviors. Almost every woman I knew could make what felt like a sound case as to why her adulterous lifestyle was good. In many cases, the women even felt like they were fixing something that was broken in our generation. One woman would reason that all men were "dogs" and that her participation in the destruction of that man's marriage was payback for him being the two-timing devil that he was. In other words, some women do NOT like nor want the men they are sleeping with! They want to intentionally destroy their marriages and, at the same time, they enjoy sleeping with them. This is literally sleeping with the enemy.

Another woman would reason that some woman had stolen her boyfriend or husband, so it had to be okay for her to do the same to another woman. In other words, she was using the man she was seeing to get revenge against another man. His wife simply got caught in the crossfire.

Some women reasoned that by sleeping with married men, they didn't have to worry about being the "main woman" or having to deal with their guys full-time. They could get sex and money from their lovers, and then send them home to their wives.

Each woman was a slave to her own reasoning; she was a concubine who strayed from her many husbands. She'd shared a piece of herself with her many lovers and they'd all imparted a piece of themselves in her. She was tired of being the informal wife and she wanted to find a man who would formally marry her. This is the reality of the adulteress. She is a graveyard of souls and an open pit for blind men who are led astray by the lusts of their dead flesh. Again, I was her so I understand the heart, mind and intentions of the immoral woman. At the same time, ever since my deliverance, God has helped me to better understand what I was, how I got that way and what would have happened to me had I not repented.

I was a concubine. I was a slave to my thinking and a slave to the many lovers I had. I lacked wisdom, knowledge and understanding and that was what made me poor enough to be "purchased." I didn't wear my lovers' last names or their rings because I was irrelevant! This is the truth that I had to tell myself to get fully free. A woman has to understand and accept what she is, where she is and what got her there before she can embrace true deliverance.

When I did get officially married, it was only after I gave my life to Christ. Nevertheless, I gave Him my life, but I didn't fully give Him my heart at that time. That's why I tried to enter holy matrimony without the holiness. This sealed the destruction of that marriage. My ex husband wasn't fully at fault. Sure, he wasn't saved nor delivered, but he didn't exactly have a fully delivered wife either. I was emotional, argumentative and manipulative ... all which are the signs that the woman in question is soul-tied to other people.

Consider the story of David and his first wife,

Michal. Michal was Saul's daughter and she
loved David when they got married. She even
helped him escape from her father when he
was trying to kill him. Nevertheless, after
David's escape, Saul gave his daughter to
another man whose name was Palti. David
went on to marry other women, but after the
death of Saul, he demanded that Michal be
returned to him. He made his demands to
Saul's son, Ish-bosheth. Ish-bosheth was now
king of Israel and David was king of Judah. To
bring peace between both nations, David said
that he wanted Michal back and Ish-bosheth
fulfilled his demands. Of course, Michal's
husband wasn't happy and he protested
David's decision, albeit unsuccessfully. When
Michal returned to David, everything was good
at first until she saw him dancing for the Lord.
The Bible tells us that it was then that she
began to despise him. Why did she despise a
man she'd once loved? It's simple. She had
two husbands. A woman's heart cannot be
portioned out to multiple men; otherwise, she

will love one and hate the other. The same goes for men. Most men who have had multiple wives would oftentimes love one and ignore the others. The rest would be nothing but tools for gratification, slaves and opportunities for them to bear more sons. The same goes in many polygamist nations today. You'll notice that once David married Bathsheba, there is no mention of his other wives. Why was Bathsheba mentioned as queen instead of his other wives? She wasn't his first wife, nor was she the first woman to bear a son for him.

Many modern-day concubines enter relations with men hoping that they will someday become their wives. This includes the ones who enter relationships with legally married men. Howbeit, our customs today give both men and women the choice to be together and to break up. We cannot (legally) force another human being to be with us. In Christianity, we no longer use purity cloths. Many women learn the hard way that a man who comes in looking for pleasure will run away when he is confronted by responsibility. This means that the many biblical laws that people think were designed to demean women were actually designed to protect them. Jacob could not walk away from Leah legally. He made her his wife when he slept with her AND he got her father's permission. Leah had a maidservant who also became Jacob's wife (Zilpah), but she was referred to as a concubine because she was a slave. The point is ... there has to be a clear distinction made in the beginning of a relationship as to the roles each party is to operate in. God wants us married (and faithful) to our spouses. As a woman, I advise women to understand the role each man is asking them to operate in, even if he doesn't verbally reveal it. The truth is ... most men will eventually clarify what it is that they are seeking from a woman. It is not uncommon for a man to meet a woman and not be sure as to what role he wants her to operate in. In such relationships, if the woman does not "test the spirit" as the Bible tells her to, she may find herself being strung along by a man who's still looking for his "main wife." Of course, she should avoid sexual immorality at all costs, but at the same time, it is always better that she understand her role with him; that way, she doesn't become his concubine by default. A lot of women spend years in relationships with men who don't see them as being worthy of being called a (formal) wife. They have children with these men and invest in them, only to discover that they are the modern-day equivalent of a concubine.

Additionally, I advise men to fully know what it is that they are looking for before they approach women and initiate a relationship with them. It is always good if a man knows the condition of his own heart. When a man's heart is right with God, God conditions his heart to seek his wife. When a man's heart is not right with God, Satan conditions him to seek women who will come in and act as wives.

Satan conditions him to look for as many concubines as possible because the devil wants to use him to hurt women and he wants to use women to hurt him. When men enter illegal, ungodly relationships, they oftentimes produce children who won't have the luxury of having them around. This produces hurting children who, like Ishmael, are cast away from their fathers and sent to live in the wildernesses of their mothers' broken hearts. They have to endure the rejection of their fathers and some have to endure being raised by a mother who is bound by unforgiveness. This sounds easy, but it isn't. They are repeatedly subjected to pain and brokenness and Satan will use this pain to disciple them into his kingdom (if they are not healed and witness a demonstration of true love).

The truth is that Satan knows how valuable a man's children are, even when that man doesn't see it himself. As a matter of fact, the men of old understood this and that's why they sought to have as many children as possible. Children back then represented posterity, wealth and power. Remember God's promise to Abraham. He said, in Genesis 22:17-18, "I will surely bless you, and I will surely multiply your offspring as the stars of heaven and as the sand that is on the seashore. And your offspring shall possess the gate of his enemies, and in your offspring shall all the nations of the earth be blessed, because you have obeyed my voice" (ESV). Nowadays, Satan has perverted the minds of many in our nation and now children are often seen as walking and talking child support payments. Satan has truly distorted man's view and definition of what a blessing is and what a curse is not.

Demonic Expansion

One of the ways that Satan encourages men to pursue seductresses is by teaching them to objectify women. By objectifying women, a man is able to manipulate, have sex with and abandon women; even if they are pregnant when he walks away. Why is this? He has learned to see them as objects designed to give him pleasure. But for this to happen, his conscience had to be seared. Naturally, our consciences would not allow us to take advantage of other human beings unless we learn to not see them as human. To do this, we start classifying and labeling people in accordance with our understanding (or lack thereof) of each class or label. For example, a racist person has learned to objectify people of a different race because he or she lacks understanding regarding the people who do not look or behave like himself or herself. To cause a person to become racist, Satan plays on that person's lack of knowledge. He then causes that person to only focus on the negative behaviors that are common to a particular race. This causes the racist person to profile certain races, and when this happens, the person will not be able to love, understand or empathize with people who are not like himself or herself. This is the objective of human objectification.

The same happens with promiscuous men. Satan teaches them to objectify women by using:

- their lack of understanding regarding women
- their dysfunctional relationships with their mothers or legal guardians
- their failed relationships
- their peers

Lack of Understanding

We cannot deny this truth: men and women

are different. Our differences are noticeable and conflict often arises between us when we do not understand each another. For example, when I counsel married couples, one of the biggest issues I've found is that women spend too much time trying to make their husbands more sensitive and open for emotional conversations. In general, most men hate dealing with negative emotions, however, women have learned to be more open with their feelings because women are emotional creatures (this is because women deal with a host of fluctuating hormones each and everyday). The husbands, on the other hand, tend to want their wives to be a little more masculine ... even though they don't specifically request that. They want their women to enjoy football games and do some of the things that they normally do with their male friends. So what ends up happening is the wives unknowingly attempt to emasculate their husbands and the men unknowingly attempt to defeminize their wives. Nevertheless, the wives want their husbands to retain the characteristics that make them manly and the guys want the women to retain the characteristics that make them girly. In other words, both spouses are trying to find a way to create what they believe to be the perfect spouse. Of course, this behavior is mainly associated with young couples because of their lack of understanding.

When a man lacks understanding regarding women, he will focus on the negatives of the female gender. In most of these cases, a man with this mindset was raised by an emotional, abusive, promiscuous or irresponsible woman. Such men often look for their mothers in their mates, which can translate to them constantly entering relationships with women who have the same demons that their mothers (or legal guardians) have or had. They will focus on "types" of women and will generalize all women according to the type that they keep finding themselves attracted to. This is evidence of demonic oppression. Lack of understanding only helps people to profile the people who are not like themselves. On the other hand, a man who was raised by a loving, responsible and attentive mother or guardian will be more patient, understanding and positive towards women.

Dysfunctional Relationships with their Mothers or Legal Guardians

A broken relationship between a man and his mother is oftentimes the catalyst behind his promiscuity and lack of empathy towards women. Let's face it. His first view of the female gender was tarnished by his mother or whomever it was who raised him. There are many men who were born into homes where their mothers were either absent, neglectful, abusive, condescending, unforgiving and hateful. In most cases, men who were born to women like these or who were placed in the care of such women will learn to objectify, mistreat and misuse women because their views of women were skewed.

Their Failed Relationships

A cycle of failed relationships can often be traced back to a failed relationship between a son and his mother or legal guardian. Men who were raised by broken women will often find themselves attracted to broken women. This leads to a series of broken relationships, all of which help such men to develop ungodly theories about women. This is because they don't realize that they're broken, so they deflect their issues onto the women they romantically link themselves to.

Their Peers

The truth is, broken men tend to surround themselves with other broken men, some of which are more broken or less broken than they are. In these relationships, they tend to fuel one another's beliefs that women are designed to be used, but not loved.

My ex's friends were mostly men who saw
women as objects (this should have been a
warning to me). They were promiscuous and
proud. One of the common denominators with
most of them was that they'd come from
broken homes. What I noticed with them was
that, like most people, they wanted to be loved
and they wanted to love someone. However,
their negative views towards women clouded
their judgments, so they repeatedly mistreated
and abandoned decent women, while falling in
love with women who were more broken (and
promiscuous) than they were. They would
always try to love the wrong women because
they did not know what love was. Needless to
say, their relationships with those women
would end and they'd re-enter the dating world
with a vengeance. They'd objectify women all
the more and the cycle would continue. They'd
find their way back in a group setting where
they'd spew their negative venom towards the
female gender, not knowing that they simply
keep dating the same demons in different

women.

Objectifying human beings is not new. Just like a racist will profile and objectify a certain race, serial killers often target a certain gender, race or age group based on their own personal views of that group. Many serial killers are captured because they focus on a "type". This helps police to monitor them and predict their next move. For example, some serial killers target prostitutes, drug addicts and runaways. When this happens, FBI profilers are often able to begin a narrowing process where they'll be able to effectively determine the killer's age range, race and family background. Most men who kill drug addicts and prostitutes were likely born to mothers or brought up by legal guardians who were drug addicted prostitutes.

The objectification of women not only hurts women, but is a trap that the enemy uses to ensnare men. You see, a man who objectifies women (and does not repent) will likely never

find his God-appointed wife; he will never know
what's it's like to be truly loved; he will not
value or stick around to raise his own children
and he will never know what it's like to obtain
favor from the Lord. He will not leave an
inheritance for his children's children and his
name will not be remembered once he's left
Earth. Instead, his life will be filled with pitfalls (a
seductress, biblically speaking, is referred to as
a pit) and regrets.

When a man falls into the trap of an immoral
woman, he will be bound by her until he frees
his soul from her through repentance and
renunciation. How so? He will remain "one"
with her, which means what's in her (demons)
will have continued access to him, even after
he's broken up with her. Here's something to
consider: Remember, we've already established
that soul-ties create a bridge between the
people who are bound by them and this allows
demonic spirits to travel from one soul to
another at will. If an immoral woman continues

to create soul-ties with men, this would mean
that she will continue to pick up new demons
from every romantic relationship she enters.
This would also mean that the demons she's
picked up from her new lovers will suddenly
have access to her former lovers if they have
not repented and released themselves from
her. This may sound far-fetched, but it's true.
Additionally, this helps us to understand
demonic expansion.

A bound man will need to free himself from
every ungodly soul-tie he's entered so that he
can cut ties with every demonic spirit that has
access to him through those ties. Some men
are still being attacked from relationships that
ended over twenty years ago! Their marriages
are failing and they don't know why. They
can't seem to progress in life, so they feel
stagnant, lost and incomplete. The issue may
be an ungodly soul-tie.

To better understand how it works, let's refer

to that soul-tie as a shopping center that links several stores (souls). The immoral woman (we'll call her Rhonda), in this case, is the shopping center and the man (Brian) is just another store on the inside of her. Every demon that is in her or has access to her will be able to go from one store (man) to the other, shoplifting at will. Brian eventually decides to end his relationship with Rhonda and the two go their separate ways.

Twenty five years later, Brian is married and has three children with his wife. He hasn't had any contact with Rhonda for more than 25 years, but everywhere he goes, he sees women who remind him of her. This is the evidence of an ungodly soul tie that has not been severed.

Brian's marriage is on the rocks. His children are rebelling against him; his workplace is threatening to lay him off and he's been having health issues. Brian, however, is a Christian man who loves the Lord, but he cannot understand why bad things keep happening to him. What Brian doesn't understand is that he's still a part of Rhonda's shopping center and every demon that shops in Rhonda has access to him through her. Brian ended his relationship with Rhonda more than 25 years ago, but what he didn't know was that he hadn't ended his relationship with the demons that came in through that relationship. To free himself, Brian will need to verbally renounce that relationship. How will he know to do so?

Let's say that Brian keeps having dreams about Rhonda. This isn't necessarily a familiar spirit coming to make him start thinking about Rhonda again. This may be the Lord telling him that he needs to free himself from her! Again, it may sound far-fetched, but there's no harm in praying about it or giving it a try. What Brian needs to do is go before the Lord and renounce that relationship. He may have already repented for all of his sins when he got saved, but he still needs to sever the soul ties between himself and his former lovers. I always tell people that when I got married the second time, I repented for having disobeyed God by unequally yoking myself to an unbeliever. God forgave me and this washed away my sins, but it did not wash away the man I was married to. In other words, repentance cleans up our spirits, but it does not clean up the mess we've made of our lives.

Brian will need to renounce the soul-tie with Rhonda and ask the Lord to divorce them. He may even need to be delivered from the demonic spirits that came in through his relationship with Rhonda as well as the ones who led him into that relationship. Once this is done, he will likely see a huge change in his life, his health, his finances, his marriage and his relationship with his children.

On one of my conference calls, I was midway through a one-on-one deliverance with a woman when the demons that were in her suddenly began to speak. One demon said, "There are sixty-two men in here! Sixty-two! Soul-ties!" With that, it began to laugh. I wasn't completely surprised; after all, I've been teaching this for years since the Bible specifically says that the two shall be one. This is not a misinterpretation or misrepresentation of scriptures because it goes on to say in 1 Corinthians 6:16 (ESV), "Or do you not know that he who is joined to a prostitute becomes one body with her? For, as it is written, 'The two will become one flesh.'" We've also established that sex is what unites two people in God's eyes, since traditional marriage ceremonies did not occur until two hundred years after the death of Christ Jesus.

When that demon said that there were sixty-two men "in there," it wasn't saying that the men were dead and burning in the lake of fire. It was saying that it had created a mass grave of sorts for those men. They were in captivity, even though physically, they appeared to be free. The demons were referencing those men's souls (mind, will and emotions). They were saying that they still have the ability to influence the minds, choices and emotions of those men because they still had access to them! The pit being referenced here is the place of captivity, which of course, was the woman who'd successfully captured them.

Proverbs 9:13-18 (NASB): The woman of folly is boisterous, she is naive and knows nothing. She sits at the doorway of her house, on a seat by the high places of the city, calling to those who pass by, who are making their paths straight: "Whoever is naive, let him turn in here," And to him who lacks understanding she says, "Stolen water is sweet; and bread eaten in secret is pleasant." But he does not know that the dead are there, that her guests are in the depths of Sheol.

Proverbs 7:25-27 (KJV): Let not thine heart decline to her ways, go not astray in her paths. For she hath cast down many wounded: yea, many strong men have been slain by her. Her house is the way to hell, going down to the chambers of death.

Just for reference, the word "Sheol" is synonymous with the words "hell" and "grave". Even though we've been taught that hell is the lake of fire, this isn't true. The Bible says that hell will be tossed into the lake of fire (see Revelation 20:40).

Now we can better understand how the objectification of women is very dangerous. It not only causes men to further inflict wounds on the women they lie with, but also causes them to fall into agreement with demons. How so? Demons have agreed to hurt those women and when a man comes along and decides to lay with them, he is being used by demons to further "expand" their influence in that woman, and expand their kingdom. With each tear in her heart, she will find herself becoming more and more desperate for love and this desperation can lead her to make some poor choices. Satan will then send men after her who say that they love her, but in truth, they will only objectify her. She has no true identity to them, other than the fact that she's a woman. With each new breakup, she will become even more broken and even more desperate. At the same time, with every new soul tie, the demons in her will gain access to more men. The men will then go and link themselves with other women, thus giving those demons access to them. It's similar to how a sexually transmitted disease spreads. This is how demons build mini-malls and massive shopping centers for themselves.

The Way of Escape

1 Corinthians 10:13 (ESV): No temptation has overtaken you that is not common to man. God is faithful, and he will not let you be tempted beyond your ability, but with the temptation he will also provide the way of escape, that you may be able to endure it.

Many mighty men of old were seduced and either overcome or almost overcome by an immoral woman (Samson, Solomon, Ahab, David, and even the first man himself, Adam). Consider each man's position.

Samson- The Spirit of the Lord was upon Samson so mightily that he tore apart a lion with his bare hands. He could not be bound by ropes; plus, he struck down one thousand men with the jawbone of a donkey. Nevertheless, Samson's weakness was women and it would take a beautiful, seductive Philistine woman named Delilah to do what an entire army couldn't do: bring him down.

David- David was the second king of Israel and his love for many women preceded him. David was said to be a man after God's own heart and God favored him; nevertheless, David's lustful heart led him into the arms of Bathsheba (Uriah's wife). After David's illicit affair with Bathsheba was about to be exposed (she'd become pregnant), David decided to place her husband, Uriah, in the front-line of battle so that he could be killed swiftly. In God's rebuke to David, He said that David could have had any (available) woman that he wanted, but he'd chosen to go after another man's wife.

Solomon- Solomon was the third king of Israel. According to the Bible, Solomon was the wisest man to ever live. Nevertheless, he did a foolish thing. He disobeyed God and married women from nations that the Lord had forbidden Israel to intermarry with. His wives turned his heart away from God and he began to worship other deities (demons).

Ahab- Ahab was the seventh king of Israel. He had everything most men could ever want: riches, power and the ability to choose any single woman that he desired. Nevertheless, Ahab chose to marry an evil Phoenician woman named Jezebel. Jezebel was so evil that they've named demons after her.

Adam- Adam was custom created by God and had no wants, needs or complaints to bear. He lived in the Garden of Eden and all he had to do was obey God and enjoy every blessing that God had provided for him. Nevertheless, Adam's wife, Eve, had been deceived by Satan and she'd disobeyed God by eating a fruit from the Tree of the Knowledge of Good and Evil. She then took a fruit to Adam and he bit into death unknowingly. That fruit was one of the most poisonous fruits that has ever been in existence.

As you'll see with each man, they had no reason to fall into temptation. They had what most men wanted; nevertheless, temptation causes a man to focus on what he doesn't have versus what he does. Satan perverts a man so that he can see what God hasn't done for him as opposed to what God has done. This is why God hates murmuring and complaining. When the Israelites murmured and complained, they caused what was supposed to be an eleven-day journey to become a forty-year journey. They focused on where they were as opposed to focusing on what God had delivered them from and where He'd promised to take them to.

Temptation tests us all, but unfortunately, most people fall into its snares because it is hard for us to be satisfied with what we have when we know that there's more out there to be had. In this chapter, I am going to address the men and the women separately so that you won't end up being used by the devil as bait, or worse, being devoured by the enemy.

To the Women

Seduction was what I knew. I had only seen one demonstration of true love in my youth and that was the love between my paternal great-grandparents. I was five or six years old when they died, but for whatever reason, my memory of them is centered around their love for one another. After their passing, I found myself surrounded by broken hearts, broken relationships and perverts.

My maternal grandmother left my grandfather to be with his best friend. I was young when this happened, but I remember the rip in the family that it caused. I remember the pain my granddad suffered through because he'd lost his wife and the mother of his six children to a man he regarded as his dearest friend. I saw the lasting effects of adultery, idolatry, lust and ungodly imaginations. My family was ripped apart by scandals, familiar spirits and ungratefulness. I watched a generational curse play out and at one time in my life, I operated

under it. I thought I needed a man to be happy.
Nevertheless, Satan used my warped thinking
to lead me into what could have potentially
been many deadly situations. I can't lie to
myself. Satan tried many times to kill me, but
God protected me. After all I've gone through, it
is amazing that I still have my right mind. I
didn't appreciate this fact until I got into
deliverance ministry and saw the toll that rape,
molestation and dysfunction had taken on some
women. I saw women battling with
schizophrenia, bipolar disorder and a host of
other demons (because that's what they are)
and some of them hadn't even been through a
tenth of what I'd gone through. Nevertheless,
God kept me through it all, and for that I am
forever grateful to Him.

God called me while I was still in the midst of
my sins and He led me to safety. I made many
mistakes in my journey, but amazingly enough,
God brought me through the brokenness and
He raised me all over again. This time, I was

raised by a protective and loving Father who not only taught me my worth, but demonstrates it to me time and time again.

My way of escape was the truth. I stopped trying to avoid it. I stopped trying to justify being the way that I was and I started acknowledging that I needed to be set free. I told myself what I was. I told myself that the men in my past had used me, despite the flattering lies I wanted to believe. I learned to handle the truth and I didn't like what I'd become. I didn't like being a pride-filled whore ... because that's what I was. Sure, it may be harsh for some people, but for me, the truth was potent enough to make me want out of the ungodly lifestyle that brought on the ungodly labels. I sought the heart of God and when I messed up, I didn't allow my fall to keep me down.

Like most people, I would occasionally lie to myself to make me feel better about myself, but

as I grew in the Lord, I stopped catering to my
emotions. I went looking for messages that
made me face the hard truth. At the same
time, I was honest with myself about what I
wanted. I wanted to be loved ... sincerely and
genuinely loved. Contrasting where I was with
where I wanted to be helped me to realize that
the path I was on would never lead me to the
love I so desperately hungered for.

The more I got to know God, the more I wanted
to please Him. Before long, the old Tiffany had
died and a new creature had been born. That's
when God took me back to His original plans for
me, plans that hadn't changed, even though I'd
gone in the wrong direction. He began to teach
me who I am in Christ Jesus. I learned to reject
the woman I'd learned to be to embrace the
treasure I was designed to be. God introduced
me to myself and He took me through a
process of letting go of what I'd picked up along
the way. At times, the process was difficult,
but I was more than determined to let it all play

out and I'm glad I did.

When God delivered me from seduction, I can honestly say that I spent some time not knowing who I was. At times, I felt confused, lost and without an identity, but I remained prayerful so that God could complete the work in me that needed to be completed. I stopped trying to figure things out and I just let God be God.

To be delivered from the wiles of the enemy, you have to do the following:

1. **Pray:** God wants to hear from you. Tell Him what it is that you are afraid of and tell Him what you want. He wants you, but you have to want Him in order for your relationship with Him to blossom.

2. **Confess your sins to God:** This was one of the hardest things for me to do because I'd tried over the years to convince myself that what I was doing wasn't wrong because I had good

intentions. Nevertheless, I had to admit to God that I was a sinner who needed Him; I had to confess my sins and fears to Him. When I did, He delivered me.

3. **Testify about what God brought you through**: Revelation 12:11 reads, "And they overcame him by the blood of the lamb, and by the word of their testimony; and they loved not their lives unto the death." You'd be amazed how much freedom is in your testimonies.

4. **Repent**: To repent isn't to apologize. It means to renounce the sin you were in and turn back to God. It means to rededicate your life to the Lord. Some people don't get free because they keep apologizing, but they never repent.

5. **Be honest with yourself**: Honesty will actually speed up the process because you won't have to go through one storm after the other just to finally accept the truth.

6. **Prepare to make sacrifices**: The

journey back to you is going to likely be filled with "drop offs" where you'll have to drop some folks off just to find yourself. Some people know who you once were and they will never let you get to who you are designed to be. That's why you'll need to sacrifice some friendships and family relationships to advance forward.

7. **End all associations with men who are romantically linked to you or are trying to romantically link themselves to you:** One of the biggest mistakes I've seen some women make is trying to redefine their relationships with certain men in order to justify staying connected to them. For example, some women will re-title their exes as "friends" just to keep them around.

8. **Throw away every "gift" <u>Satan</u> has given you in exchange for your sin:** The items your exes gave you were offerings from Satan. If you want God's

best for you, you need to give up everything that you acquired through or because of your sin (except the children, of course).

9. **Rid your life of the altars that you once lied on:** I've told many people to do this and many of the ones who did have testified about how the blessings suddenly began to flow in their lives. If you fornicated on your bed, get rid of it. This may sound extreme to some, but if in doubt, simply pray about it. I've heard people justify keeping the stuff, saying things like they couldn't afford a new bed and they continued to struggle year after year. Then again, I've witnessed some people who, despite their financial realities, decided to rid their lives of everything that tied them to their pasts, and their lives changed for the better emotionally, financially and spiritually.

10. **Never allow yourself to want anything more than you want God:** God said to,

"seek ye first the Kingdom of God and all
His righteousness, and everything else
will be added to you." (See Matthew
6:33). I didn't understand what that truly
meant for a large portion of my life, so I
put my wants and needs first. I thought
that I could get God on board later, so I
acquired relationships and things, only to
lose them all. Anything you put before
God is an idol, but if you put God first, He
will give you relationships and things
that Satan doesn't have the power or
legal right to take from you.

Don't allow the media to tell you how to look or
determine your worth. Find yourself in Christ
and let God introduce you to the treasure who
you are. Additionally, don't let Satan use you
as bait. Sure, we all have gone through some
things in life, but it is what you do with those
experiences that will determine whether you
have victory over them or if those experiences
have victory over you. Understand this: When

Satan uses women as bait, he doesn't intend for them to have lifelong relationships filled with love, joy and the peace that surpasses all understanding. He will only let a man foster a temporary relationship with you so that the man can break you all the more. Additionally, he wants to use you to capture that man so that he can devour him. God's way is the better way; it's the only way that will produce the results that you want.

To the Men

Because of the pain I'd suffered, I allowed the enemy to use me. I didn't understand what I was doing back then. I only knew where I wanted to be and I took the shortcut I believed would help me to get there faster. I knew that God wasn't pleased with my life, but I thought to myself that I'd be able to make it up to Him later. God had to bring me out of that darkness and once I came out of it, I realized how close to death I'd come. Additionally, I had the misfortune of losing two of my maternal uncles because of immoral women.

One of my uncles had been married for more than a decade (I believe) to his wife and it was common knowledge throughout our family (and their city) that his wife had carried on numerous adulterous affairs. She'd even had a child with another man, but despite it all, my uncle would not walk away. We begged him to leave because, as women, we understood the danger he was in. You see, adulterous women can be very dangerous when they want another man.

My uncle's wife put him out and moved another man into their house the very same day he left. He moved into another property that he had and I knew that he was hoping to reconcile with his wife. I was 24 years old then and my uncle and I had just started communicating with one another.

Over the years, that particular uncle had been

absent for the most part of my life because the family didn't support his marriage. He was ashamed because he'd told his siblings about his wife's numerous affairs, but after each one, he'd reconciled with her. He called me one day and as I was talking with him, my heart began to ache. He was telling me about how he'd gone to his old home to fix the washing machine. He laughed as he talked about how his wife's new guy couldn't do anything. Suddenly, I started crying and I said to him that they (his wife and her new lover) were going to kill him. I will never forget his response. He said, "I know." He also told me that he had all of his insurance and property going to his children when they turned eighteen. I tried to explain to him that she could file a motion in court and the court would likely grant her access to everything, but he was confident that she couldn't get anything.

A week or more after my uncle moved out, his wife sent their then three year old son to live with him. Not long after that, his house caught on fire in the middle of the night. He died saving his son's life. Now, I can't pin his death on his wife, so I won't say or imply that she or her lover is responsible for it. No one was never charged with the crime and the Fire Marshall ruled that the fire started because of faulty wiring (not a surprising ruling, given that it was a small town in Mississippi). That meant there was no criminal investigation. Nevertheless, what I can say is ... I knew I was about to lose my uncle and I warned him. I didn't know who I was in Christ back then, but I said to him what was laid upon my heart heavily. If I could go back, I would have interceded for him.

A couple of years later, his youngest brother was killed by the police. He believed that his wife was having an affair and the two had gotten into an argument. Of course, I don't know the details, but what I do know is that my uncle was intoxicated and his wife told him to leave. He refused, so the wife called the police.

The police came and my uncle was outside hiding behind a parked car. Anyhow, when they told him to come out, he did, but according to the officer who shot him, he had his hands in his pocket. My uncle was shot five times by that officer. Of course, he was unarmed. And just recently, my deceased uncle's son with that same woman was shot and killed by her boyfriend for allegedly disrespecting him.

Again, I can't completely point fingers at the wife without knowing the whole story, but I can truly say that had my uncles given their lives to Christ and let Him choose their wives for them, I believe they'd still be alive today. As you can see, my family was torn to pieces by seduction, adultery and murder; these were some of the demons that came after my grandfather and his bloodline. Of course, I had to be delivered from those generational curses. I had to renounce the curses in my bloodline, uproot every demonic seed my ancestors planted and I had to get a new heart and a new mind. The old me had to die so that a new creature could be born.

Don't give your vigor, power, wealth or seeds (children) to immoral women. An immoral woman can spend years with you and have children with you, but this won't change what she is or what her assignment is in your life. I warn men to this day that a woman can spend years with a man that she does not want and she will tolerate that guy until something seemingly better comes along. When another man enters the picture, her husband's life will be in danger.

You don't need to just be delivered from the immoral woman; you need to avoid her path altogether. Here are some tips to help you avoid her:

1. **Pray:** Praying often is communicating with God and activating your ears to hear from Heaven. You need a consistent prayer life if you want to

avoid the many snares that Satan has set for you.

2. **Confess your weaknesses to God**: God knows where you're weak and He knows where you're strong. All too often, people boasts on their strengths, while the devil plays on their weaknesses. Be honest with God. Tell Him where you need His help the most and then, let Him work on you.

3. **Repent**: Repentance has three parts: acknowledging your sins, regretting your sins and turning away from your sins. People often get apologizing confused with repenting, and for this reason, they keep falling into the same pits time and time again.

4. **Divorce your type**: Your type is the type of demons that keep coming after you (example: Jezebel, Delilah, Athaliah, Lust, Premature Death, etc.). Repent of your sins, and then sever every ungodly soul tie and familiar spirit that's

connected to you (see prayer at the end of this book).

5. **Prepare to make some sacrifices**: Anytime you want to advance in God, the Lord will show you what and who's been keeping you bound. You must be willing to let go of certain things and certain people to move forward in God.

6. **Learn to love yourself**: God told husbands to love their wives as they love themselves. Howbeit, many men love many women with a false and perverted love called lust. The reason for this is they don't love themselves. When you learn to love you, you will not want to share yourself with an immoral woman. God will never send you a godly woman to love when you don't love yourself, because you won't know how to differentiate her from the ungodly women of your past.

7. **Change the channel**: Much of today's media is demonic. The Bible tells us to

guard our hearts. We do this by understanding how we are created. Your eyes are doorways and your ears are gateways to your heart. You have to guard them if you want to guard your heart. You should not be listening to music that promotes lust, perversion, lasciviousness, fornication, violence, pride, rebellion, or any behavior that goes against the Word of God. Additionally, you shouldn't be watching movies that promote sin. Fill yourself up with valuable knowledge. When driving, for example, utilize that time to listen to encouraging (godly) music, godly sermons and audio books designed to help better your life (informative messages that promote the sale and marketing of real estate, self-advancement, etc.). Live by this rule: If you don't want it coming out of your life, don't let it come in your ears or eyes.

8. **Seek God above yourself:** God has to

be first and that's why He said that we are to seek the Kingdom of God first. We can never place God in the backseat if we expect Him to drive. Anything you place before God (including self) is an idol and all idols have to be destroyed.

9. **Confront and bind the devil in your life:** Demons encourage sexual immorality and a host of sins. They do this so they can enter your life and get behind the wheel of your choices. They also do this to keep you from every blessing that God has set aside for you (a godly wife, children, success, etc.) Confront every demon that's bound you and take authority over it. You are the officer and you can arrest (bind) them, and then you can cast them into prison (the pit). If you don't know how, read articles and watch videos online regarding self-deliverance (from a Christian perspective). There are also many great books that teach self-deliverance.

10. **Ask God for your wife:** This prayer will shake some things up in your life because everything that's been assigned to keep you from your wife will begin to reveal itself. Additionally, every person the enemy sent to keep you from your wife will begin to reveal himself or herself. This is just how advancement works. You were designed to advance, but Satan perverted you and taught you to retreat instead. Ask God to prepare you for and introduce you to the wife He has assigned to you, and then prepare yourself for the changes He will make in your life. Make up your mind that you won't abort the process; instead, let God do what He wants and needs to do in your life so that you can advance in Him. When there's no lust in your heart, the immoral woman has no power over you. When she yields the power of the temptress, you will be able to yield the power of the Holy Spirit. Always remind yourself that she is a beautifully

disguised death trap and by doing this, you'll be able to walk by her without feeling the need to look at or engage with her lustfully.

Matthew 5:28 (NIV): But I tell you that anyone who looks at a woman lustfully has already committed adultery with her in his heart.

If you are already in the clutches of an immoral woman, you have to free yourself from her grip by praying down lust, idolatry and ungodly imaginations. You also need to do the following:

- Sever every ungodly soul-tie that you have with her. You do this by verbally renouncing those soul-ties after, of course, you've repented to God for entering them.
- Renounce your relationship with her and the devils that brought you two together.
- You can't ask her to go away; you have to send her away! End the relationship, but be kind about it. If she insists on

calling or coming by your house, you may need to block her number, change your phone number or get a restraining order if necessary.

- Get rid of any and everything she's ever given you. Believe it or not, some people stay bound because they hold on to material things. Those things keep them from moving on. Additionally, you need to understand that in witchcraft, witches often need a point of contact; meaning that they need something of yours to perform their evil magic or they need to place something in your possession.

- Find new places to visit. If she knows the places you visit, she may show up there to see, provoke, or attack you.

- Each day, rebuke every evil word that she has spoken (or is still speaking) about you until God gives you the clearance to stop.

- Pray and ask God to cover you with the

blood of Jesus daily.

- Pray for her deliverance. The worst thing you can do to a demon is ask God to free the person whom it has bound. That person came in your life to bind you. How ironically disappointing will it be to the enemy when God uses you to free that person instead?

How to Handle Temptation

Let's examine the story of Joseph and Potiphar's wife.

Genesis 29:6-13 (ESV): Now Joseph was handsome in form and appearance. And after a time his master's wife cast her eyes on Joseph and said, "Lie with me." But he refused and said to his master's wife, "Behold, because of me, my master has no concern about anything in the house, and he has put everything that he has in my charge. He is not greater in this house than I am, nor has he kept back anything from me except you, because you are his wife. How then can I do this great wickedness and sin against God?" And as she spoke to Joseph day after day, he would not listen to her, to lie beside her or to be with her.

But one day, when he went into the house to do his work and none of the men of the house was there in the house, she caught him by his garment, saying, "Lie with me." But he left his garment in her hand and fled and got out of the house.

One of the things that should interest you is the fact that Joseph fled; meaning that he ran out of the house. Joseph didn't walk away; he ran away. Why did Joseph run? The following scripture will sum it up for you.

1 Corinthians 6:18 (ESV): Flee from sexual immorality. Every other sin a person commits is outside the body, but the sexually immoral person sins against his own body.

The Bible doesn't tell us to "walk away" from sexual sin; it tells us to run away from it. Joseph ran because he didn't want to give place to the devil. He knew that his flesh could rise up and he could have easily sinned against God had he stayed there and reasoned with the woman. Before she grabbed his garment, Potiphar's wife had repeatedly asked Joseph to sleep with her, but he simply told her no and kept working. He responded to her in the very same manner that Jesus Christ responded to Satan when he took Him up on a mountain and tempted Him. Jesus answered Satan when he tried to persuade Him to turn stones into bread, throw Himself off the pinnacle of a temple and finally, when he tried to get the Lord to worship him. You'll notice that the moment Satan told Jesus to worship him, Jesus didn't just respond; He sent him away.

Matthew 4:8-11 (ESV): Again, the devil took him to a very high mountain and showed him all the kingdoms of the world and their glory. And he said to him, "All these I will give you, if you will fall down and worship me." Then Jesus said to him, "Be gone, Satan! For it is written,

"'You shall worship the Lord your God

and him only shall you serve.'"

Then the devil left him, and behold, angels came and were ministering to him.

When Potiphar's wife asked Joseph to sleep with her, Joseph answered her and spoke of the goodness of her husband to her, but when she tried to provoke Joseph's flesh, he ran. Why did he run? Because she was in her own house, so he could not throw her out. Additionally, Joseph wasn't a foolish man. He knew that if he stayed there and tried to reason with her, he could have been tempted. God provided him with a way of escape in the form of a door and he ran out of it.
1 Corinthians 10:13 (ESV): No temptation has overtaken you that is not common to man. God is faithful, and he will not let you be tempted beyond your ability, but with the temptation he will also provide the way of escape, that you may be able to endure it.

Sometimes, you just have to run from your

tempter and let everyone who judges you because you ran say whatever they choose to say about you. It is better to run away from temptation than it is to fall into it. Some people end up bound because they keep trying to maintain an ungodly reputation. Let it go! The people who celebrate your sin are the same people who are celebrating your decline. You see them cheering you on, but in truth, their cheers are deceptive.

Proverbs 27:6 (NASB): Faithful are the wounds of a friend, But deceitful are the kisses of an enemy.

You confront temptation by running away from it, but you do not run from the devils in it. You confront and bind them whenever they decide to come against you. Never miss the door that God has opened for you to escape through. The worst thing that can happen to you is that the door shuts and you find yourself alone in the darkness with an immoral woman. Sure, you may enjoy her momentarily, but her sting is long-term.

Note: By the grace of God, I've been blessed to come across a few old friends (and former enemies) who were once immoral women. Some of them have gotten saved and are now serving the Lord ... some are even in leadership. What's amazing to me is many of these women were as deep in the trenches of sin as I was—or deeper! It goes to show that there is no level so deep that God's long hand can't reach. God is willing to set free anyone who is willing to allow Him.

Praying Down the Stronghold

Below, you will find four prayers:
- Prayer for men who want to avoid the seductress.
- Prayer for men who want to free themselves from a seductress.
- Prayer for women who want to be set free from the spirits behind seduction.
- Prayer for women who want to release the men they've captured while operating as a seductress.

Please note that while the prayers may be similar, they are different.

Prayer for Men who want to Avoid the Seductress

Dear Heavenly Father,

I come before you today repenting for all of my sins, both known and unknown. I ask that you forgive me for my sins and deliver me from the oppression that my sins have brought upon me. I renounce fornication and every form of sexual immorality. Lord, you said that if any man be in Christ Jesus, he is a new creature and old things are passed away. You said all things would be made new. I ask that you make me new again. Set me free from the strongholds of my sin. I renounce lust, sexual immorality, lasciviousness, rejection, divorce, abandonment, and every sin that has had me bound. I repent for the sins of my ancestors and I renounce all generational curses, oaths and sins up to fifty generations on both sides of my family.

Lord, I ask that you order my steps in your Word. Keep me from the path of the immoral woman. Lord, lead me to the wife you have set aside for me. Prepare my heart for her and teach me to be the husband you have designed me to be. Open my eyes and let me see people the way that you see them. Keep me from the path of the Oppressor and fill me with your precious Holy Spirit. I break every ungodly oath I've entered and I revoke every ungodly word and prayer that's been sent out by me or against me. I blind every demonic eye peering into my life and I cast down every ungodly plot, plan and scheme that the enemy has sent out against me. I command every familiar spirit and every demon operating in my life to leave me now and to never return. I render the plans and plots of the enemy null and void and I obstruct the paths of every immoral woman headed my way.

I revoke every demonic assignment against my seed (future children) and my children. Lord God, I ask that you keep and guide me. I need you and I submit myself to you.

In the name of Jesus Christ, I pray.

Amen.

Prayer for Men who want to Free themselves from a Seductress

Dear Heavenly Father,

I come before you today repenting for all of my

sins, both known and unknown. I ask that you forgive me for my sins and deliver me from the oppression that my sins have brought upon me. I renounce fornication and every form of sexual immorality. Lord, in my sin, I have joined myself to an ungodly woman. I repent for my relationship with her and I ask that you set me free from her and every demon, power and principality that has been operating in and through her. Lord, I turn my heart back to you and I ask that you be the head of my life from this day forward.

I renounce lust, sexual immorality, perversion lasciviousness, rejection, divorce, hatred, abandonment, and every sin that has me bound. I repent for the sins of my ancestors and I renounce all generational curses, oaths and sins up to fifty generations on both sides of my family. Lord, sever the soul tie between me and (say her name or their names). I renounce those soul ties and everything that entered my life through them.

Lord, I ask that you order my steps in your Word. Deliver me from the path and snares of the immoral woman. Lord, lead me out of the darkness into your perfect light. Order my steps and lead me to the wife you have set aside for me. Prepare my heart for her and teach me to be the husband you have designed me to be. Open my eyes and let me see people the way that you see them. Keep me from the path of the Oppressor and fill me with your precious Holy Spirit. I break every ungodly oath I've entered and I cancel every ungodly word and prayer that's been sent out by me or against me. I blind every demonic eye peering into my life and I cast down every ungodly plot, plan and scheme the enemy has sent out against me. I command every familiar spirit and every demon operating in my life to leave me and to never return. I render the plans and plots of the enemy null and void and I obstruct the paths of every immoral woman headed my way.

I cancel every demonic assignment against my

seed (future children) and my children. Lord
God, I ask that you keep and guide me. I need
you and I submit myself to you.
In the name of Jesus Christ, I pray.
Amen.

Prayer for Women who want to be Set Free from the Spirits behind Seduction

Dear Heavenly Father,

I come before you today repenting for all of my
sins, both known and unknown. I ask that you
forgive me for my sins and deliver me from the
oppression that my sins have brought upon
me. Lord, today, I acknowledge that I am a
seductress and I repent for my sins against you
and your people. You said in your Word that
whom the Son (Jesus) has set free is free
indeed. Lord, you said that if we confess our
sins that you are faithful and just to forgive us
for our sins and cleanse us from all
unrighteousness. Lord, I confess my sins to
you on today and I ask that you cleanse me.

Lord, set me free every ungodly spirit operating in and through me. I renounce and divorce any ungodly spirit-husbands that I may have and I renounce lust, adultery, fornication, pride, lasciviousness, greed, idolatry, seduction and every demonic spirit operating in my life. I bind those spirits and command them to leave my life in the name of Jesus Christ.

Lord, deliver me from temptation and make me new again. Let me be pleasing in your eyes. Deliver me from every ungodly soul-tie that I've entered, and prepare me for the husband you have for me. Drive away any man who may enter my life and try to impersonate the man you've assigned me to. I want you and I need you. Lord, I want to be kept by you.

I obstruct every ungodly bridge that allows the enemy to cross over into my life and I blind the eyes of every demonic agent peering into my life. I revoke every ungodly word I've spoken and every ungodly prayer I've prayed. I cancel every ungodly word that has been spoken against me and every ungodly prayer that's been sent out against me. I cancel every demonic assignment against my womb, my children and my future children. I will not be a vessel of darkness, nor will I lead men into temptation.

Lord, I want what you have in store me for and not what the enemy has. Please guard me, protect me and lead me. Keep me from the paths of ungodly men and teach me the difference between godly and ungodly men. Cause me to see men the way you see them.

Keep me, Lord and do not allow lust or any demonic force to re-enter me. I ask these things in the name of Jesus Christ.
Amen and Amen.

Prayer for Women who want to Release the Men they've Captured with Seduction
Dear Heavenly Father,

I come before you today repenting for all of my sins, both known and unknown. I ask that you forgive me for my sins and deliver me from the oppression that my sins have brought upon me. Lord, today, I acknowledge that I am a seductress and I repent for my sins against you and your people. I release every man from the promises and oaths he has made to me. I forgive every man who has hurt and abandoned me and I release them to you now.

Lord, deliver me from temptation and make me new again. Let me be pleasing in your eyes. Deliver me from every ungodly soul-tie that I've entered and prepare me for the husband you have for me. Drive away any man who may enter my life and try to impersonate the man you've assigned me to. I want you and I need you. Lord, I want to be kept by you.

Lord, set me free every ungodly spirit operating in and through me. I renounce and divorce any ungodly spirit-husbands that I may have and I renounce lust, adultery, fornication, pride, lasciviousness, greed, idolatry, seduction and every demonic spirit operating in my life. I bind those spirits and command them to leave my life in the name of Jesus Christ.

I obstruct every ungodly bridge that allows the enemy to cross over into my life and I blind the eyes of every demonic agent peering into my life. I revoke every ungodly word I've spoken and every ungodly prayer I've prayed. I revoke every ungodly word that has been spoken against me and every ungodly prayer that's been sent out against me. I revoke every demonic assignment against my womb, my children and my future children. I will not be a vessel of darkness, nor will I lead men into temptation.

From this day forward, Lord, I choose you. Help me to put you first in my life and to keep you first. I also ask that you deliver every man from me who I may have trouble releasing and

also deliver them from the hands of the enemy.
Deal with their hearts and cause them to
hunger for you, Lord. Draw their hearts to you
and help them to be the vessels you've
designed them to be for your glory.
In Jesus's name I pray,
Amen.

*Note: Be sure to go to a deliverance ministry,
but pray and ask God to show you which one
He wants you to go to. There are some
ungodly establishments disguised as churches
and you don't want to end up in one of them.
That's why it's necessary to pray first and to
hear back from heaven before going.*

Random Facts

Below are some little known (or unpopular) facts that should help you on your journey.

1. An immoral woman has a devil or several demons in her. That's why it is important that we learn to discern not just who we are talking with naturally, but who we may be having a conversation with supernaturally. If you ever witness her going through deliverance from demons and the deliverance minister commands those demons to talk, you'd be amazed at how they had been using her.

2. In the southern states, as well as other places, a woman who has had several husbands to pass away is a woman said to have a "white liver." Such a woman is said to be a "nymph" or have

a highly insatiable sex drive. The truth of the matter is, the women like this have what is called a spirit-husband. It is him who keeps "knocking off" her husbands. He had to get her into sin so that any man who found her was also in sin or had to come into sin to get her. Sin puts a man's life within his reach. After that man became one with her, he unknowingly created a bridge between her and the spirit-husband that she had and this gave that demon access to that man and his life.

3. When a man sleeps with an immoral woman, he unknowingly becomes one of her rapists. He victimizes her, even though she willingly had sex with him. How so? He becomes a part of the men Satan is using to break her all the more and keep her in the lifestyle she's in. Additionally, because of sin, she is not in the sound mind that God has set aside for her.

4. An immoral woman isn't always immoral because she wants to hurt people. Sometimes, she's just a lost soul in search of love. The best thing a man could do for her is to love her enough to not touch her.

5. Many immoral women are addicted to sex, but their addiction has little to nothing to do with the pleasure and the orgasms that sex produces. All too often, it is centered around the passion in sex. This passion makes her feel loved, if but for a moment. Some are addicted to the sounds that a man produces in sex because it makes them feel like they're good at something. Others are addicted to the compliments they get during and after each sexual encounter.

6. America and other nations promotes condom usage, rather than abstinence. This is because the condom-makers average over a billion American dollars

annually. Trojan alone makes close to half a billion dollars.

7. Demons do not respect condoms. They'll pass from one person to the next, even if his semen is left behind.

8. When a man gets sexually involved with an immoral woman and he is faithful in regards to wearing condoms, he is not safe. He will more than likely become the father of one or more of her children because an immoral woman understands the psyche of a man. She knows that the man in her life will religiously wear condoms and if she doesn't object to it, he will slowly begin to trust her. He will come to think that, like himself, she does not want to have children at that point in her life. One day, he will likely find himself spending several hours with her and he will have only brought one condom. He will use his only condom, not realizing that they will likely have sex several times that

day. Believing that the woman he's lusting after does not want children at that stage in her life, he will try to do what Onan did (see Genesis 38:8-10). He will try the withdrawal method. After seeing that she didn't get pregnant, he will begin to trust her all the more, and slowly, but surely, he will have more unprotected sex with her. One day, she'll discover that she's pregnant and he will abandon her. This will start a vicious cycle of rejection and abandonment in the life of his child.

9. More than 80 percent of men have admitted to manipulating their lovers so they wouldn't have to wear a condom.

10. More than 50 percent of women who play the adulteress do not want to spend their lives with the men whose marriages they are attacking. They simply want the pleasure of knowing they won.

11. There are specific types of demons

assigned to sexual warfare and most of them are what is commonly referred to as marine spirits. They include, but are not limited to: mermaid spirits, Leviathan (a demon behind pride) spirits, spirit-spouses (spirit husbands/ spirit wives), etc.

12. Spirit-wives are the demons who often link themselves to men and are responsible for most sexual dreams and sperm emissions while asleep. Like spirit husbands, they are incredibly jealous and will not allow a man to have a long-term relationship or a successful marriage. They are also behind impotency and other male-related problems.

13. When a woman dresses seductively, despite what she says, she is fishing. She may be fishing for other men, fishing for compliments, fishing for redemption behind a broken relationship ... either way, she is fishing. As such, she

becomes demon bait.

14. This little known fact was taken from Health.Harvard.edu: "Men who have marital partners also live longer than men without spouses; men who marry after age 25 get more protection than those who tie the knot at a younger age, and the longer a man stays married, the greater his survival advantage over his unmarried peers." Married men are said to live at least 17 years longer than their unmarried counterparts.

15. Some women sleep with married men because of how the men they are involved with rank in their eyes and in the eyes of society. They don't feel they can "pull" a man of their adulterous lovers' ranking if that man were single, so they go after high-ranking married men. This is because in their hearts, it is better to be the whore of a king than the wife of a peasant. At the same time, they know that should their lovers

abandon them, they can likely get a monetary payout or be able to control those men by threatening to tell their wives or expose their evil deeds.

Made in the USA
Coppell, TX
28 December 2021

70306631R00219